Thespian Theology

Advent, Christmas, Epiphany
Cycle A

John A. TenBrook

CSS Publishing Company, Inc., Lima, Ohio

Scripture quotations are from the *New Revised Standard Version of the Bible*, copyright
1989 by the Division of Christian Education of the National Council of the Churches of
Christ in the USA. Used by permission.

For more information about CSS Publishing Company resources, visit our website at
www.csspub.com.

ISBN 0-7880-1845-0   PRINTED IN U.S.A.

I dedicate this book to Bitty, my wife/companion/lover of 36 years, who has always been an icon of Jesus for me ... and who has endured my humiliating goofiness with great good humor all these years.

Table Of Contents

Advent Preface

Advent, like much of Christian practice, is totally counter-cultural. While the world, summoned by the marketing mavens of Madison Avenue, begins celebrating "the Christmas season" as soon as Halloween is over, we Christians are summoned by Advent to *remember*, to *reflect*, and to *wait*.

Remember the past ... While store windows throughout the land are adorned with snow and miniature Dickensian villages, we remember the coming of the Anointed One, 2,000 years ago. We remember Mary: a young peasant girl who had the courage to say, "Yes," to the outlandish proposal of a plan to change the world forever. And we remember John the Baptizer: a strange, intense mountain man who, thirty years after his birth, pointed the way to the Lamb of God.

Reflect on the present ... While innumerable mail order catalogues and websites summon us to an orgy of "holiday gift-giving," we reflect on the coming of the Redeemer into our hearts in the mundane here and now. We are summoned to ask ourselves: Am I ready for him? Is my celebration of the Incarnation truly appropriate to the occasion?

Wait for the future ... While the world parties as if there's no tomorrow, we contemplate apocalyptic literature in the sure and certain knowledge that, while no one knows the day and time of his return, Jesus is coming back.

So, Christians don't have much fun during Advent? Wrong.

Christians always have fun. We serve a God whose great desire is "that my joy may be in you, and that your joy may be made full" (John 15:11).

Fun ... This book of Advent homily/dramas is all about fun. As you use this thespian theology — either in place of a Sunday homily or just for fellowship and laughter — my prayer is that you will remember, and reflect upon, a God who had such a wonderful sense of humor that he created you (and me).

Advent 1
Isaiah 2:1-5
Romans 13:8-14
Matthew 24:37-44

N-o-o-o-t Exactly ...

Thespian Theological Thoughts

Have you seen the Hertz television ad where a group of businessmen are having a series of bad experiences with a rental car? The boss asks his subordinate if he rented from Hertz, and the subordinate says, "N-o-o-o-t exactly." That's the little gimmick in this play: it's just a drawn out "not" ... not "newt." The purpose of this silly little mnemonic device is to remind us that we can't put God in a box. Every time we think we have him figured out, he says, "N-o-o-o-t exactly!"

The when and the where of his return — the Day of the Lord — has been a subject of speculation since the day Jesus ascended. Peter, James, and John thought it would happen during their lifetimes — and that was two millennia ago! And every time a Napoleon or a Hitler or a Pol Pot comes along, someone decides that the antichrist has finally come, and therefore the end times are upon us.

And God quietly says, "N-o-o-o-t exactly!"

As my son-in-law continually tells my grandson, "You have to wait." And in waiting, you (and I) have to stay alert and be ready. And that means laying aside the deeds of darkness and putting on the armor of light — and owing nothing to anyone except to love one another (Romans 13:8).

Cast

Narrator
Larry Last-Days
Darryl Doubtful
Priscilla Peace-and-Joy
Jesus

Props

Sign: "Jesus Is Coming!"

Sign: (mathematical calculations)

(Narrator enters stage right, carrying sign: "Jesus Is Coming!" Narrator moves to stage left and sets down the sign)

Narrator: That great and wonderful Day of the Lord: men will hammer swords into plowshares; nation will not lift up sword against nation ... and they "ain't gonna study war no more, Lord, ain't gonna study war no more!" When, O Lord? When will those last days be? Or are we *already in* those days? Lots of folks have wondered about these questions for lots of years. Take my man, Larry Last-Days.

(Larry Last-Days enters stage left, picks up sign)

Larry: There's no need to wonder ... we *are* in the last days! Brothers and sisters: I have made a thorough study of scripture and prophecy, and if my calculations are correct (*and I am sure they are!*), Jesus is coming back next Tuesday at 3:14 p.m.

Narrator: Is that Eastern Standard Time or Pacific?

Larry: (*Picks up board on which a complicated set of equations are scribbled*) Let's see now ... Actually, it's Mountain Standard Time, 'cuz he's coming down at Vail, Colorado.

Narrator: I see ... well, you'll pardon me if I don't hold my breath until then.

Larry: Just you wait ... You'll see ... you'll see. (*Exits stage left, leaving sign and calculations behind*)

Narrator: On the other hand, we have some folks who are equally convinced that there *never will be* a Day of the Lord. Meet my man, Darryl Doubtful.

(*Darryl Doubtful enters stage right; picks up sign and calculations board*)

Darryl: 3:14 p.m. next Tuesday, on top of Mascara Mountain ... yeah, right! (*Shakes his head*) Larry: what a moron! Ya know, bozos like Larry have been predicting the end of the world for centuries now: they would read tea leaves or chinchilla entrails or something, and they'd come up with some exact time and place when Jesus is comin' back. Then they'd go off to a mountain and wait ... and nothing would happen! I'm *doubtful* that Jesus is *ever* coming back: he doesn't want to have to deal with morons like Larry! (*Sets down sign and calculations; exits stage right*)

Narrator: And someplace in the middle, we have the folks who believe in Jesus, but they don't spend any time thinking about the Day of the Lord ... or even about the Lord himself. Speaking of which, heeeere's Priscilla Peace-and-Joy!

(*Priscilla Peace-and-Joy enters stage left; picks up sign and calculations*)

Priscilla: Now what's this? (*Reads calculations*) Oh, really! (*Shakes her head*) I don't know why Larry wastes his time worrying about such things as when Jesus is coming back. All I know is: Jesus told us not to try to figure it out, so I'm not spending *one minute* of my time thinking about it. Besides, I'm just too busy having fun, in the peace-and-joy-and-love-of-the-Lord! (*Sets down sign and calculations; exits stage left, singing "Peace-and-joy-and-love!"*)

Narrator: Hmmmmm ... well, that's another point of view. (*Pauses*) Tell ya what: let's fast-forward in time to Tuesday afternoon at 3:15.

(Larry, Darryl, and Priscilla enter: Larry is very upset; he picks up his calculations; Darryl struts about, proud and pleased with himself; Priscilla dances around, singing softly)

Larry: I don't understand it! I used Revelation and the writings of Nostradamus and Jeanne Dixon ... and all my calculations added up.

Darryl: I told you, moron: Jesus isn't coming back!

Voice of Jesus: *(From offstage)* Don't be too sure about that, Darryl!

Darryl: Huh! Who dat?

Jesus: Who do you think it is, Darryl?

Darryl: I'm afraid to say it.

Larry: *(Pokes Darryl in the chest)* It's Jesus, moron!

Jesus: No, it's Jesus *Christ!*

(Darryl runs upstage right, and tries to hide)

Larry: See? I told you so. He *is* coming back ... I just missed it by a few minutes, huh, Lord?

Jesus: N-o-o-o-t exactly ...

Larry: Well, then, when *are* you comin' back, Lord?

Jesus: That's not for you to know, Larry.

Priscilla: See? I told you so, you moron. We're not supposed to know, and we're not supposed to think about it, huh, Lord?

Jesus: N-o-o-o-t exactly ...

Priscilla: What do you mean?

Jesus: You are not to know when I will return ... but that doesn't mean you are not even to think about it. You must stay alert, and be ready, for I may return at any time.

Larry: See? I told you so, you airhead. By trying to figure out when he's coming, I'm staying alert and being ready, huh, Lord?

Jesus: N-o-o-o-t exactly ...

Larry: But, but, but ...

Jesus: Larry, my child: Staying alert and being ready for my return doesn't mean spending all your time trying to figure out something which God alone knows.

Priscilla: See? I told you so.

Jesus: Excuse me, Priscilla, my child: Paying no attention and going your selfish way is *not* staying alert and being ready, either.

Larry and Priscilla: How then shall we live, Lord?

Jesus: Lay aside the deeds of darkness and put on the armor of light!

Larry and Priscilla: Huh?

Jesus: Do the right thing! Stop doing the things you know are wrong. No more strife and jealousy, you two! Live your lives in witness to my love, which lives in your hearts. Love your neighbor, and you will fulfill the law.

Larry: I'm sorry I called you an airhead, Priscilla. Forgive me?

Priscilla: I'm sorry I called you a moron, Larry. Forgive me?

(*Larry and Priscilla hug each other*)

Jesus: There's one more important thing you two need to do, if you want to fulfill the law.

Larry and Priscilla: What's that, Lord?

Jesus: Look at Darryl over there. (*Larry and Priscilla turn upstage toward Darryl*) He's scared and confused about all this. Go and tell him about me, so that he won't have anything to be scared and confused about.

(*Larry and Priscilla go to Darryl; they pick him up and hug him*)

Jesus: Because I *am* coming back!

Larry and Priscilla and Darryl: Pretty soon, Lord?

Jesus: N-o-o-o-t exactly!

Advent 2
Isaiah 11:1-10
Romans 15:4-13
Matthew 3:1-12

Phil Pharisee
And The Baptizer

Thespian Theological Thoughts

Hey, one conversion out of four isn't too bad for an itinerant evangelist, right?

The premise of this play is that *some* of the self-righteous religious leaders may have heard and responded to what John the Baptizer was saying. We don't know that it happened this way — but neither do we know that it didn't happen.

John came to call God's people to repentance and righteous (fruitful) living, and perhaps some of the religious establishment heard and responded to John, as Nicodemus heard and responded to John's cousin.

How many of us today — we who consider ourselves religious leaders — truly hear and respond to God? Do our lives produce fruits of righteousness and obedience? Or are we consumed by our head-knowledge of scripture (Phrank Pharisee), or our social status (Stu Sadducee), or just plain old macho superiority (Sam Sadducee)? Can we, like Phil Pharisee, look at this wild-eyed, counter-cultural Judean baptizer, listen to him ... and pay attention?

A production suggestion: Either before or after the play, you might want to share Don Francisco's "Steeple Song" with your audience. It's on Benson CD02456: *Don Francisco — The Live Concert*. The message of this song is the Baptizer's message.

Cast

Narrator
John
Crowd (3-4)

Sam Sadducee
Phrank Pharisee
Stu Sadducee
Phil Pharisee

Props/Costumes

John — fright wig, scruffy clothing, lunch pail, honey, plastic
container labeled "locusts"
Crowd — blanket, rocks
Pharisees and Sadducees — dark clothing, clerical collars
Phrank Pharisee — t-shirt: "PIT"

(When the play begins, the Narrator is at stage left and the Crowd is seated on a blanket, center stage)

Narrator: Now in those days, John the Baptizer came, preaching in the wilderness of Judea.

(John enters stage right, carrying a lunch pail containing a plastic container labeled "locusts" and a jar of honey)

John: Repent and get right with God, because God and his kingdom are at hand!

Crowd: (*In unison*) Lord, I am a sinner! Wash me clean!

(John pantomimes baptizing each Crowd member)

Narrator: John was a weird dude: I guess you could say he was a first-century Palestinian hippie. He lived in the wilderness and he never visited a barber.

(John scratches his wig)

Narrator: He ate wild honey and locusts — and I don't think they were your gourmet chocolate-covered locusts from Starbucks.

(*John opens his lunch box and takes out locusts and honey and eats*)

Narrator: John made the friendly neighborhood religious establishment very nervous.

(*Enter Pharisees and Sadducees, stage left. They remain in a group downstage left*)

Sam Sadducee: Who does this ding-a-ling think he is, anyway? "The voice of one crying in the wilderness," indeed! What's that supposed to mean?

Phrank Pharisee: It's from the prophet Isaiah, and it's about the messenger of God's Messiah.

Sam: Isaiah! Now there's another nut-case. A lovely poet he was, but a nut-case nonetheless.

Phil Pharisee: Sam, you've gotta give this John the Baptizer some credit. People are flocking to him from everywhere. His numbers are up, and ours are down! Maybe we ought to listen to him.

Stu Sadducee: Oh, horsefeathers, Phil! What could a hippie from the hills have to say to *us*?

Phil: We'll never know unless we listen, Stu.

(*Pharisees and Sadducees turn and look at John*)

John: (*Points to Pharisees and Sadducees*) You bunch of snakes! What brings you slithering down here? Did somebody warn you that you're in big trouble, or are you just here because this is where the crowds are?

Sam: What did I tell you? He's a nut-case, and a disrespectful one at that!

Stu: (*Points his finger at John*) You can't talk that way to us: we are sons of Abraham! And besides, we're all on the Board of Trustees at the Jerusalem Country Club. If you ever want to amount to anything, you'd better treat us with respect!

(*Members of the Crowd stand up and grab edges of their blanket. There are stones in the blanket; Crowd pulls the blanket up, to bounce the stones up and down*)

John: I tell you this: God can make these *rocks* into children of Abraham. Being a child of Abraham doesn't mean squat! What matters to God is the way you live your life, not what country club you belong to!

Phrank: Now see here, young feller. My name is Phrank Pharisee, and I am Chancellor of the Pharisee Institute of Theology. (*Opens his coat to reveal a t-shirt which says "PIT"*) I have studied scripture all of my life. How *dare* you lecture *me* about what matters to God?

John: "PIT," huh? That's very appropriate, Phrank — because the Pit Of Hell is exactly where you're headed for, if you don't clean up your act.

Phrank: Well, I never!

John: That's right, Phrank: You're *never* gonna see the kingdom of God unless your life begins to bear good fruit.

Sam: Fruit? What are you talking about, dipstick?

John: I'm talking about repentance and righteous living, Sam: getting right with God!

Sam: Well, why don't you say so, you moron? Why all this blathering about *fruits*?

Phil: I think what he's saying, Sam, is that our lives are like trees which bring forth fruit, and that the fruit of our lives should be righteous, if it is to be set before a holy and righteous God.

John: You're catching on, Phil! But there's more.

Stu: Well I, for one, don't want to hear any more! My life — or my "fruit," or whatever — is quite satisfactory, thank you very much: I'm a faithful church-goer, and my kids are all honor-roll students.

John: Doesn't cut the mustard, Stu. If your life is nothing but deadwood, it gets chopped down and thrown into the fire, my man.

Stu: Where do you get the right to tell me that my life is deadwood, you spaced-out hippie?

Sam: Yeah! And where do you get the right to come "baptizing" all these simple folks, and telling them their sins are washed away?

John: I'll tell you this, Sam: I am washing people with plain ol' H-Two-O, for repentance ... but someone is coming after me — and he's the Main Man. I'm not fit to carry his golf clubs. He will change people from the inside. He'll baptize people with the Holy Spirit and with fire.

Sam: That sounds like *pain* to me. No thanks!

John: Your choice, Sam. And your choice, Phrank and Stu and Phil. But know this: The one who comes after me is really going to clean house. He's the real deal! He's going to place all the righteous fruit before God ... and the rotten fruit he will throw into a fire that can never be put out!

Sam: Aw, horsefeathers! You can't scare me, John. Hippie God-freaks like you are a dime a dozen. Adios, sucker. (*Exits stage right*)

Stu: Me, neither! I'm outta here: I'm late for a board meeting at the club. (*Exits stage left*)

Phrank: Well, I'll tell you one thing: We'll be discussing you at the next P.I.T. faculty meeting, and you'll be hearing from us, you wild-eyed rabble-rouser! (*Exits stage left*)

Phil: You know, John, some of what you're saying is making some sense to me. (*Puts arm around John*) I'd like to have you meet my cousin Nicodemus: he's a thoughtful guy.

John: (*Starts walking off stage right*) Okay, Phil. And I'd like to have you meet *my* cousin. (*Gives the audience a knowing look*) He's a *life-changing* guy!

(*John and Phil exit together*)

20

Advent 3
Isaiah 35:1-10
James 5:7-10
Matthew 11:2-11

The Prophet Has His Doubts

Thespian Theological Thoughts

Jesus said that John the Baptizer was more than a prophet: He was a prophet of prophets, the one whom Malachi described as making the road smooth for the coming of God's Messiah. Among those born of women, Jesus said, none has appeared who is greater than John. And yet, this prophet of prophets, this towering figure of biblical history, this blood relative of Jesus — has his doubts!

A prophet of prophets with feet of clay.

Hey, put yourself in John's place: you've devoted your life to doing the work God gave you to do; you baptized everybody (including Jesus) who came to you; you have continued, boldly and unashamedly, to speak the truth; you know the scriptures intimately, and you believe that God will be faithful to his promises to redeem Israel and bring his kingdom to pass ... but now you've been thrown in Herod's dungeon, and you know what happens to folks who get thrown in Herod's dungeon! Might you not begin to entertain some doubts about the future?

And look at Jesus' response to John's questions and doubts: He doesn't just say, "Of course I'm the Messiah, John; you know that!" Instead, Jesus points to the fruits of his life on earth: the blind see, the deaf hear, the lame walk, and the poor hear the Good News of God's kingdom.

When the world wants to know if we follow Jesus today, they need to see and hear the same from and about us.

Cast
Narrator
John

21

Herod
Guards (2)
Dan Disciple
Doug Disciple
Jesus
Followers (6)
  Blind
  Lame
  Leper
  Deaf
  Dead
  Poor

Props
  John — Bible
  Herod — Burger King crown
  Guards — spears

———————————

Narrator: Prophets: those weird, outspoken little guys who run around speaking God's truth. We say that we admire them, but when all is said and done, we really don't like prophets, do we? Because we really don't like the *truth!*

(*Herod enters stage left; John enters stage right*)

Narrator: Ol' King Herod had a problem with a prophet,
A problem with a prophet had he —
The prophet said that Herod was a-livin' in sin,
And Herod answered, "No, not me!"

John: Herod! Hear God's truth: Herodias, the woman you are fooling around with, is not your wife. She is the wife of your brother Phil, Herod, and the name of that tune is *adultery!* You're the king of Israel, Herod: You can't be doin' this, bubba! (*Shouts*) Give it up, Herod, and get right with God!

22

Herod: I don't want to hear this. (*Shouts*) Guards! (*Guards enter stage left*) Take this misguided miscreant and lock him in the dungeon. It's bread and water and no contact visits for you, bubba!

(*Guards rough John up, and lead him off, stage right*)

John: Hey, watch it! Don't mess up the camel's hair.

Herod: That oughta fix his little red wagon. (*Exits right*)

Narrator: So the king locked up the man whom Jesus described as "more than a prophet." In fact, Jesus said that, "Among men born of women, there has not risen anyone greater than John the Baptizer."

(*Guards enter with John; they throw him down center stage and exit right*)

John: Oh, maaan! What's goin' on here? I'm just doing my job — telling the truth and preparing the way for the Messiah — and they throw me in the slammer! (*Picks up a Bible and starts reading*) I thought Isaiah promised that "the wilderness and the desert will be glad." And that "the recompense of God will come and he will save you." And that "the ransomed of the Lord will return with joyful shouting." Maaan, I don't feel like doing any joyful shouting in this dump!

(*John's Disciples enter stage left; it's dark in the dungeon and they're having a hard time seeing*)

Dan Disciple: Man, it's dark in here. I'm scared!

Doug Disciple: John, are you in here?

John: Doug? Dan? Is that you? I'm over here!

(*Doug and Dan find John and come to him*)

Dan: What happened to you, man?

John: I guess I ran afoul of the Man, Dan. Ol' Herod couldn't deal with my telling him he had to quit foolin' around with Phil's wife ... so he locked me up!

Doug: What can we do to help you, John?

John: Hmmmm ... well, you know what, guys? Gettin' locked up has made me start thinking about this whole Messiah thing. Wouldn't you think that if Jesus really is the Messiah, he could get me out of here? (*Shows them his Bible*) I mean, look at all the wonderful things Isaiah wrote about the coming of the kingdom of God. When is that good stuff gonna happen to *me*? I'm just rotting here in prison!

Dan: What are you saying, John?

John: I'm saying that I'm wondering if this Jesus is the real deal. I want you to go and ask him if he's the one, or if we are to expect somebody else.

Doug: John, you're our main man! You're the premier prophet. Are you telling us that *you* are having doubts about Jesus?

John: I'm scared, Doug ... and I just want to know, okay?

Dan: That's some heavy stuff, John. If *you* are having doubts, I guess *we* need to find out for ourselves.

Doug: We'll go find Jesus and ask him, John. God bless you, man! (*Dan and Doug exit stage left*)

(*Jesus enters stage right, accompanied by Followers; they move downstage, and Jesus pantomimes ministering to Followers, who are seated around him*)

24

Narrator: Meanwhile, Jesus was continuing to preach and live the Good News of God's kingdom.

(*Dan and Doug enter stage left and move toward Jesus*)

Dan: Jesus! Herod has thrown your cousin John in prison.

Doug: John sent us to ask you, Jesus: Are you the Messiah of God, or shall we look for someone else?

Jesus: I am sad to hear about what happened to John, and I can understand his fears and doubts. Go and tell John what you see and hear in the streets:

(*Jesus' Followers stand up one by one and deliver the lines joyfully*)

Blind: The blind receive sight ...

Lame: The lame walk ...

Leper: Lepers are cleansed ...

Deaf: The deaf hear ...

Dead: And the dead are raised up ...

Poor: And the poor — that's all of us — have the Good News preached to them!

Jesus: And blessed is the one who keeps from stumbling over me.

Dan and Doug: Then you are saying...?

Jesus: I am saying: You will know that I am authentic by the fruits of my life. (*Turns toward the audience*) And even today people will know that *you* are authentic followers of me by the fruits of *your* lives. So go, and do as I have done: Love the Lord your God with all your heart and with all your soul and with all your mind ... and love your neighbor as yourself!

Advent 4
Isaiah 7:10-17
Romans 1:1-7
Matthew 1:18-25

Never Give Up On God ...
God Never Gives Up On You!

Thespian Theological Thoughts

Joseph, the carpenter of Nazareth, has long been a hero and role model for me. I admire — and covet — his willingness to believe and trust God, even in the face of catastrophic and unexplainable circumstances.

Think about it, from Joseph's point of view:

• You are a respected businessman in your small town.
• You are a faithful Jew.
• You have gotten yourself a wife-to-be, and you look forward to your life as husband and father.
• Your betrothed now comes to you pregnant, with a story about an angel and the Holy Spirit of God.
• Everyone in your small town soon discovers your shameful secret, and tongues begin to wag.
• You know that the law provides for stoning as punishment for your betrothed, and you really don't want to hurt her.
• And now, an angel of God comes to you and says, "Don't be afraid — trust God!"

Would *you* be willing to trust God, rather than your feelings?

God's message in this story is one of which I must constantly remind myself: *"Don't depend on your feelings — depend on God."*

And: *"Never give up on God ... God never gives up on you!"*

Cast
Narrator
Joe
Gilda

27

Miss Marplestone
Joe's Mom
Joe's Dad
Angel
Reverend Joe
Sam Salvation
Willy Works

Props/Costumes
Joe's Mom and Dad — ping-pong paddles
Angel — halo and/or wings

———————

Narrator: This is a story of three guys named Joe. Our first Joe is a person of the teenage persuasion.

(*Joe enters stage right*)

Narrator: Poor young Joe has many of the problems that are common to persons of the teenage persuasion: Gilda, the girl-of-his-dreams, thinks he is a total geek.

(*Gilda enters stage right*)

Joe: Hi, Gilda ... nice day, huh?

Gilda: Geek! (*Exits stage left*)

Narrator: And his English teacher, Miss Marplestone, thinks he is a hopeless doofus.

(*Miss Marplestone enters stage left*)

Joe: Miss Marplestone, why did you give me a D- on my term paper?

Marplestone: Because the only thing you did correctly was spelling your name, doofus! (*Exits stage right*)

Narrator: But the *worst* problem Joe has is his parents —

(*Joe's Mom and Dad enter stage right; they pantomime arguing*)

Narrator: They argue with each other all the time, and Joe gets caught in the middle. He feels like a ping-pong ball.

(*Joe's Mom and Dad take out ping-pong paddles and hit Joe back and forth as they fight*)

Mom: You never pay any attention to our son, and that's the reason why he's a geek and a doofus!

Dad: Oh, for Pete's sake, you've spoiled the kid rotten! That's why he's a geek and a doofus.

(*Mom and Dad continue to bat Joe back and forth*)

Narrator: And finally ...

Mom and Dad: (*In unison*) I want a divorce! (*Mom exits right; Dad exits left*)

Narrator: Joe was destroyed by all this! He just wanted to ...

Joe: Give up! What's the use? My life is a total mess. I think I'm just gonna ... I don't know what I'm gonna do!

(*Angel enters stage left*)

Angel: Joe!

Joe: Huh? Who're you?

Angel: I am an angel of the Lord.

Joe: Whoa! What do you want with me, man?

Angel: I came to tell you not to give up on God, Joe. God hasn't given up on you.

Joe: Man, it sure feels like he has!

Angel: Don't depend on your feelings, Joe. Depend on God! Trust him. He loves you and wants the best for you. Trust him!

Joe: So you're really an angel of God?

Angel: Yup ... the real deal!

Joe: And you're telling me to trust God, even though I feel like my life is out of control?

Angel: That's what I'm telling you, Joe. Try it: trust God and see what happens! (*Puts his arm around Joe*)

Joe: Well, okay, I'll try it ... if you and God say so!

(*Joe and Angel exit stage right*)

Narrator: Our second Joe is the Reverend Joe.

(*Rev. Joe enters stage left*)

Narrator: He's the pastor of St. Swithin's-in-the-Swamp. Reverend Joe has his own set of problems: His tiny flock is getting tinier by the day, and the few parishioners who are left spend their days fighting and gossiping ... and generally not being a light unto the world!

(*Sam Salvation and Willy Works enter stage right, arguing*)

Sam Salvation: Willy, I'm telling you: My salvation is eternally secure! Nothing can separate me from the love of Christ (Romans 8:39), and I cannot lose my salvation ... and if you don't believe that, Mr. Willy Works, you're a moron!

Willy Works: Well, I'll tell *you* something, Mr. Sam Salvation: I am working out my salvation with fear and trembling (Philippians 2:12) ... and if you're not doing that, you are worse than a moron. You're goin' to hell on a Honda!

Sam: (*Notices Rev. Joe*) Oh, hello there, Reverend Joe.

Rev. Joe: Good morning, Sam ... 'Morning, Willy. How are you gentlemen this fine day?

Willy: Humph! That was sure a wimpy sermon you preached on Sunday, Reverend! When are you gonna set the record straight for bozos like Sam here?

Rev. Joe: Well, I ...

Sam: Bozos? Listen, moron ... I've just about had it with you! I can't continue to fellowship with this apostasy! (*Storms off stage left*)

Willy: (*Sticks his finger in Rev. Joe's chest*) And I can't put up with wimpy sermons any more: If you can't preach it like it is, I'm outta here! (*Storms off stage right*)

Rev. Joe: Lord, what am I going to do? Nobody listens to anybody around here, and try as I may, I don't seem to be able to make *anybody* happy!

Narrator: Reverend Joe was at the end of his rope. He just wanted to ...

Rev. Joe: Give up! What's the use? This church is a total mess! I think I'm gonna ... I don't know what I'm gonna do!

(*Angel enters stage right*)

Angel: Joe!

Rev. Joe: Huh? Who are you?

Angel: I'm an angel of God.

Rev. Joe: Whoa! What do you want with me?

Angel: I came to tell you not to give up on God, Joe. God hasn't given up on you.

Rev. Joe: He hasn't? I sure would've given up on me, if I were God. I feel like I'm not making any progress with these people.

Angel: Don't depend on your feelings, Joe. Depend on God. And remember, he is God — and you're not. God loves you, Joe, and he wants the best for you. Trust him!

Rev. Joe: So you really are an angel of God?

Angel: Yup ... the real deal. I keep telling you guys this!

Rev. Joe: And you're telling me to trust God, even though my life and my church are out of control?

Angel: That's what I'm telling you, Joe. Trust God. Try it, you'll see. (*Puts his arm around Joe*)

Rev. Joe: Well, okay, I'll try it ... if you and God say so.

(*Angel and Rev. Joe exit stage right*)

Narrator: And that's our story about trusting God.

(*Joe and Rev. Joe enter stage right*)

Joe: Wait a minute: I thought you said you had a story about *three* Joes.

Rev. Joe: Yeah, who's the third?

(*Angel enters stage right*)

Angel: You think *you* have problems? Joe the carpenter had a problem which no one had ever faced before: He was engaged to a young girl, and she turned up pregnant! Joe didn't do it, and his fiancee said she was still a virgin ... and everybody in Joe's little town said, "Yeah, right!" People made fun of Joe, and the law said that Joe should take her outside the town and stone her to death. Joe's life was a total mess!

Rev. Joe: And then God sent *you* to Joe, right?

Joe: And Joe trusted God, right?

Angel: Right! And it's a good thing he did, right?

Joe and Rev. Joe: Right!

Christmas Day 3 (Years A, B, C)
Isaiah 52:7-10
Psalm 98
Hebrews 1:1-12
John 1:1-14

What's The Word?

Thespian Theological Thoughts

When I was a mindless teenager (that was a few years before I became a mindless adult), I was an acolyte in a large midwestern Episcopal church. As a senior in high school, I was privileged to be one of the servers at the midnight service on Christmas Eve. When the Gospeler, an elderly and revered priest, stood up and read John 1:1-14, I was scandalized!

Where's all the warm-fuzzy stuff about the baby Jesus and the manger and the shepherds and the lambs? What's this stuff about "In the beginning was the Word," anyhow?

It took me many years to realize what John I is about — and I'm not sure I've got it all right yet! But one thing I have grasped: Jesus is "the exact imprint of God's very being."

And Christmas is really the Feast of the Incarnation. That little baby was — and is — almighty God, and he came here to redeem me.

Merry Christmas! Spread the news!

Cast

Gospeler
Norman Nativity
John The Apostle
Luke The Physician

Props/Costumes

Gospeler — t-shirt (or sign): "Gospeler"

(Gospeler enters down the center aisle, reading John 1)

Gospeler: "In the beginning was the Word, and the Word was with God, and the Word was God. He was in the beginning with God. All things came into being through him, and without him not one thing came into being. What has come into being in him was life, and life was the light of all people. The light shines in the darkness, and ..."

(Norman Nativity, who has been sitting in the audience, stands up and interrupts)

Norman: Whoa, whoa, whoa! Hold on a minute: This is Christmas! You know: Happy birthday, Jesus! Where's the story about Jesus?

Gospeler: Excuse me? This *is* the story about Jesus.

Norman: No, it's not! At least, it's not the one I want to hear. *(Quotes from Luke in the King James Version)* "And she brought forth her firstborn son, and wrapped him in swaddling cloths, and laid him in a manger; because there was no room for them in the inn. And there were in the same country shepherds abiding in the field, keeping watch over their flock by night ..."

Gospeler: Well, yes — that is a story about Jesus, and it's a lovely one, but ...

Norman: You're darn right it's a beautiful story! Why, that feller Handel even wrote a song about it. *(Starts to sing)* "There were shepherds abiding in the field, keeping watch over their flock by night ..." That's the story we want to hear on Christmas: Baby Jesus in the manger and the shepherds and the angels, and all like that! Not all this heavy theology about "the Word was with God and the Word was God." What's with that?

Gospeler: It's the story of Jesus.

Norman: Huh?

Gospeler: "And the Word became flesh and lived among us, and we have seen his glory."

Norman: Huh?

Gospeler: The Word is Jesus, and Jesus is God in the flesh, Mr., um ... what is your name, sir?

Norman: I am Norman Nativity ... and I *still* say that on Christmas we should be hearing the story about baby Jesus and the angels and the shepherds and the lambs. That's what Christmas is about, isn't it?

(*John The Apostle enters stage right*)

John: Not!

Norman: Say what?

John: Christmas, Norman, is about much more than the miraculous birth of a child to a peasant girl.

Norman: Huh? Who are you?

John: I am "the apostle whom Jesus loved."

Norman: John? Then you wrote that stuff about the Word, huh?

John: Well, God wrote it through me.

Norman: So, what are you saying about Christmas, John?

John: I'm saying that if you think Christmas is just a warm-fuzzy story about a little baby born in a manger, you're missing the point, Norman.

Norman: Huh?

John: Christmas is about what the Gospel says in verse 14 back there. (*Points to Gospeler*) Read it again, please.

Gospeler: "And the Word became flesh and lived among us, and we have seen his glory, the glory as of a father's only son, full of grace and truth."

Norman: But ... but ... but ...

John: Sounds like you left your motor running, Norm. What are you trying to say?

Norman: Well, gee ... I just love that nativity story so much, John! I've heard it on Christmas ever since I was a little shaver. It was read in the Christmas pageant when I was in the second grade: I was a shepherd, and I got to smear mud on my face and wear my bathrobe to church. My little sister was an angel. What a monumental piece of miscasting that was! Even the TV guys play that story at Christmas. It *must be* what Christmas is about!

John: Because the TV guys use it?

Norman: No ... because we're all so familiar with it.

Gospeler: As I said, Norman, the nativity is a wonderful story — and it is beautifully told in Luke, and we all love it. But do you know what Christmas is, Norman?

Norman: Huh?

Gospeler: Christmas is the Feast of the Incarnation.

Norman: Huh?

John: It's the celebration of God becoming flesh and living among us, Norman. And if we miss that fact, we miss the point of it all; Almighty, eternal God became a little baby, born to a peasant girl in a cold, dirty animal pen. The God who created everything in the universe became one of us, and lived with us, and showed us the Way and the Truth and the Life. That's why we read the scripture which you called "heavy theology." It's to remind us that Jesus is "the reflection of God's glory, and the exact imprint of God's very being." That's from my brother Paul.

Norman: Oh. So you mean I can't hear the story about the baby Jesus in the manger, and the angels and the shepherds and the lambs?

(*Luke The Physician enters stage left*)

John: I don't mean that at all, Norman. You can hear that story any time you want to. In fact, my brother Luke here will tell it to you now, if you'd like. (*Luke puts his arm around Norman, and they start to exit stage right*)

Norman: All riiiight!

Luke: But, Norm?

Norman: Yes?

Luke: Just remember who that little baby is, and why he came here, okay?

Norman: Gotchya, boss! (*Norman and Luke continue to exit stage right*) But can we sing the part about (*Sings*) "And suddenly, there was with the angel a multitude of the heavenly host, praising God, and saying, 'Glory to God' ..."

Luke: Sure, Norman. That's my favorite part also. (*They exit stage right*)

Epiphany Preface

epiphany *n.* 1. A Christian festival held on January 6 in celebration of the manifestation of the divine nature of Christ to the Gentiles as represented by the Magi.
2. A revelatory manifestation of a divine being.
3. A sudden manifestation of the essence or meaning of something.

So, we're talkin' *manifestation* here.

Manifestations of the Way, the Truth, and the Life:
- to John the Baptizer, who played Little League ball with him;
- to Simon Peter, whose hard head had a hard time getting it;
- to seven self-centered churches in "Cliqueland";
- to Wilfred, the Warden of the World's Wisdom;
- to Habakkuk, the Hebrew prophet;
- to Polly Pure and Righteous Rudy;
- to a baby Chris Chun;
- to Wilma Worrier and Fred Fretful; and
- to three single-minded sinners.

I pray that these silly homily/dramas may be vehicles by which Jesus will be made manifest to you. Please pray that Jesus will continue to be made manifest to me. Thanks, and God bless you!

Epiphany Of The Lord (Years A, B, C)
Isaiah 60:1-6, 9
Psalm 72
Ephesians 3:1-12
Matthew 2:1-2

Unfathomable Riches!
No Assembly Required, Gentiles Included

Thespian Theological Thoughts

Sincere apologies, first off, to a certain television commentator who is lightly parodied herein, and to anyone who has a special fondness for him. I do not mean to comment one way or the other about the gentleman's knowledge and love of God — he was just a handy device to begin wondering about unconditional offers.

God's offer to us is extravagant, and of course it is unconditional. And, as we acknowledge especially during the season of Epiphany, this offer is available to all people. We can all have the unfathomable riches of God's love — and it's not for what we do, but for who we are, all of us.

The world may not see it that way — but our job is to help them see, by opening their hearts and minds to the knowledge and love of Christ.

May this silly little homily/drama help someone to do just that.

Cast

TV Announcer #1
TV Announcer #2
Andy Looney
Narrator
Isaiah
David
Paul

43

Props
> Isaiah — scroll
> David — scroll

(Narrator is stationed stage right; TV Announcer #1 and TV Announcer #2 enter stage left)

TV #1: *(Shouts)* Get your Eureka Handy-Dandy cordless kiwi-fruit-slicer now, for only $29.95, plus shipping and handling. Don't delay — do it today!

TV #2: *(Rapidly, in a monotone)* Some assembly required, batteries not included, until supplies last, this offer good only in the Continental United States, offer expires December 31st. *(TV #1 and TV #2 exit stage left)*

(Andy Looney enters stage right)

Andy Looney: Ya know, what the world needs today is just a good unconditional offer.

Narrator: You think so, huh?

Andy: What? Who's that?

Narrator: It's just me: your friendly Narrator. Who are *you*?

Andy: I'm Andy Looney ... and I'm just wondering about these infomercials we see on TV all the time. Did ya ever wonder how many lawyers it takes to write all the conditions they stick on the end of every offer they make? Why, sometimes all the qualifiers at the end take more air time than promoting the product! Like I said, what this world needs is a good ol' *unconditional* offer!

Narrator: I can think of lots of good old unconditional offers, Andy.

Andy: Yeah? Like what?

Narrator: Like the one my man Isaiah made, centuries ago: This offer still stands.

(Isaiah enters stage left, carrying a scroll)

Isaiah: Arise, shine, for your light has come, and the glory of the Lord has dawned upon you. For behold, darkness covers the land; deep gloom enshrouds the peoples. But over you the Lord will rise, and his glory will appear upon you. Nations will stream to your light, and kings to the brightness of your dawning.

Andy: What kind of unconditional offer is that?

Isaiah: It's the best kind: God himself is promising his people Israel that his glory will appear upon them, and that nations will come to their light!

Andy: Hmmm ... well, ya know, God's glory and all that is very nice, but that's kinda vague. I was hoping for something a little more specific.

Narrator: You want specific? We'll give you specific! Listen up, Andy: Here's our boy David.

(David enters stage right, carrying a scroll)

David: He shall defend the needy among the people; he shall rescue the poor and crush the oppressor ... In his time shall the righteous flourish; there shall be abundance of peace till the moon shall be no more ... He shall have pity on the lowly and poor; he shall preserve the lives of the needy. He shall redeem their lives from oppression and violence, and dear shall their blood be in his sight. (*Looks at Andy and points to scroll*) Is *that* specific enough for you?

Andy: Yeah, that's pretty specific ... but it must be a conditional offer, huh?

Narrator: Why do you say that?

Andy: Because all that good stuff hasn't happened yet: There's no abundance of peace ... and, for sure, the righteous aren't flourishing! So this offer must have some conditions, and obviously we're not fulfilling the conditions!

(*Paul enters stage right*)

Paul: I've got the answer for that one, guys!

Andy: And who might *you* be?

Paul: I am Paul ... and *you* might want to listen to me, friend.

Andy: You may fire when ready, Gridley.

Paul/David/Isaiah: (*Together*) Huh? Whazzat?

Andy: Admiral Dewey at the battle of Manila Bay ... I just meant to say: "Get on with it, bubba!"

Paul: Oh. You're confusing me! Now, where was I? Oh, yes: Andy, you had a question about *conditions* on God's promises. Nothing could be further from the truth: God's offer of redemption and salvation in Christ Jesus is absolutely unconditional. And do you know what the real good news is?

Andy: No, what?

Paul: The read good news — which I've been called to shout from the rooftops — is that God is an equal opportunity promiser and fulfiller! Everybody — people like you who've never paid any attention to God, and people like Isaiah and David here who've devoted their whole lives to God — we all stand in the same place before God. He loves us all equally, and he gives us all the same unconditional offer of rescue.

Andy: But what about my earlier question? Dave, you said that the righteous are gonna flourish, and that there's gonna be peace everlasting, and that the poor will be saved, and on and on. Hey, guy, it's not happenin'! What's up here? Is this not a *conditional* promise, and we're not fulfilling the conditions, so God's not fulfilling his promise?

David: Not at all, Andy. What God is talking about here are spiritual — not material — matters. In a spiritual sense, the righteous (those who please and honor God) *do* flourish, although materially their lives may not show it.

Paul: And "peace" doesn't simply mean the absence of wars among nations. It means the *inner* "peace of God, which passes all understanding," which can rule in an individual's heart when he or she is yielded to God.

Isaiah: And God *has* had pity on the lowly and poor: He *has* redeemed their lives ... in a *spiritual* sense, and that's the most important sense.

Narrator: That is what we mean by "unfathomable riches," Andy: the spiritual richness of communion with God. And it's all yours, unconditionally: no assembly required; everyone included; supplies will last forever; no expiration date.

Andy: Well, I don't know. You've given me something to think about. But I *still* think the world needs a good unconditional offer of a kiwi-fruit-slicer! Did ya ever notice how hard it is to make a real clean slice of a kiwi fruit?

(*Andy wanders off, stage left; Isaiah, David, and Paul shrug their shoulders*)

Isaiah/David/Paul: (*Together*) Oh, well ... praise the Lord, anyway!

Epiphany 1 (Years A, B, C)
Isaiah 42:1-9
Psalm 89
Acts 10:34-38
Matthew 3:13-17 (A)
Mark 1:7-11 (B)
Luke 3:15-16, 21-22 (C)

An Epiphany For Cousin John

Thespian Theological Thoughts

Did you ever wonder what it was like growing up as a kid with Jesus in the neighborhood? After all, God-with-us did live and work and play in a family, in a neighborhood, with friends and relatives.

Including, perhaps, his cousin John.

So, it's at least possible that, when Jesus came to John to be baptized, the two men had shared family experiences. If that were so, John could have known Jesus intimately: played with him, laughed and cried with him. And it's not beyond the realm of possibility that John entertained some questions about this most ordinary — yet extraordinary — cousin of his.

I love baseball: I've played it and coached it and watched it all my life. And, for my sins, God has made me that most pitiable of all men: An eternally hopeful fan of the Boston Red Sox. I pray that you will pardon and excuse my offbeat and not-too-irreverent (I hope) use of baseball as the family experience shared between Jesus and his cousin John. Let your mind roam into the fantasy, and enjoy this play!

And speaking of fantasies: Maybe someday, in this world where all things are possible, the Red Sox will win it all.

Cast
Narrator
John
Jesus

Dove (optional)
Voice of God (offstage)

Props
John — photo album
Narrator — flip chart/magic marker

(Narrator is at lectern, stage left)

Narrator: Did you ever wonder about John the Baptizer and Jesus? I mean, these guys were cousins, right? The Bible doesn't have much to say about the childhood of Jesus, so we don't know if John and Jesus spent any time together when they were kids. But assuming they did: What do you think it would have been like to have the Son of God for your cousin?

(John enters stage right, carrying a photo album; he comes to center stage and sits down)

Narrator: Well, what do you know? Here comes John now! Whatchya got there, John?

John: Oh, I was just looking through the family photo album, and thinking about my cousin Jesus. The family's very proud of him ... they say he's the Son of God, you know!

Narrator: Yes, we know. What do you think, John?

John: Oh, I know who he is: He is God ... and I am not!

(Narrator comes to center stage and sits down with John)

Narrator: Let me look at this album, John. So, what was it like, growing up as a cousin of Jesus?

John: We had a great childhood! We played ball together: Jesus was the shortstop on our Little League team, the Lions of Judah. Here's our team picture the year we won it all. Jesus was a fantastic fielder — but at the plate, he wasn't all that great: He never struck out looking, but he was a sucker for a high fast ball.

Narrator: Really?

John: Yeah. Wouldn't you think that the Son of God would be able to bat 1.000?

Narrator: I suppose he *could have* ... but maybe he chose not to, ya know?

John: Well, I dunno ... if he chose not to, it cost us a few ball games, I'll tell you that!

Narrator: It sounds like you're having some doubts here, John.

John: Not doubts, just questions. As I said, I know who Jesus is: All my life, I've heard the story from Mom and Aunt Mary about how I jumped in Mom's womb when Aunt Mary came to visit.

Narrator: So, what kind of questions do you have, John?

John: Well ... I guess I'm just wondering about the *ordinariness* of Jesus: He was just another kid in our neighborhood. A good kid, a kid you could always depend on ... but still, he was just a kid! When he fell down and scraped his knee, he bawled, and it bled — just like any other little kid. (*Points to album*) See the bruise on his shoulder in that picture? That was a high fast ball, and Jesus didn't get out of the way in time!

Narrator: So Jesus didn't walk on water when he was a kid, huh?

John: Walk on water? Hey, he almost *drowned* when he was little: I was the one who had to fish him out! But later on, he was a good swimmer — and he was the *best* at cannonballs! But do you see what I'm sayin' here? If Jesus really is God in the flesh ... why is he so *ordinary*?

Narrator: Maybe he's ordinary to you, John, because you grew up with him ... but he's not ordinary to the rest of us!

John: Why? What do you know about him that I don't know?

Narrator: Do you have a couple of hours? It'll take me that long to tell it all ... and it still won't be complete!

John: Naaah, I've got to get back to business.

Narrator: Business?

John: Yeah, you know: baptizing. That *is* my business, after all. (*Gets up and starts to exit stage left*) Okay, you sinners: Prepare ye the way of the Lord! (*Jesus enters stage left*) Repent and be ...

Jesus: Hi, cuz! (*Pantomimes scooping up a ground ball and throwing to first base*) How's it goin'?

John: Lord Almighty! What are *you* doing here?

Jesus: I've come to be baptized by you, John.

John: But Lord: You are God, and I'm not! I should be the one being baptized by you, don't you think?

Jesus: Let's just do it, John, okay? It's right that we do this now, to fulfill all righteousness.

John: (*Turns to Narrator*) Ya see what I mean? He wants *me* to baptize *him* ... as if he needs to have any sins washed away! I mean, maybe he did strike out with the bases loaded in that game against the Cana Cubs ... but that wasn't like a *sin* or anything! Why does he need me to baptize him, fer-Pete's-sake?

Narrator: John, I can think of at least four reasons why. (*Gets flip chart and records the four points*)
> One — Jesus is confessing sin on behalf of the nation of Israel;
> Two — He is showing his support for your ministry, John;
> Three — He is beginning his own public ministry today; and
> Four — He is identifying with the sinners who repent, and showing us the way.

Jesus: That's nice theology. But why not just do it because I asked you to, John?

John: Okay, Lord, if you say so! (*Leads Jesus downstage center; they pantomime baptism*) I really don't know what to say here, Lord.

Jesus: Don't talk, John: Listen!

(*Optional: A small child, dressed in white as a bird, runs across the stage, flapping wings*)

Voice of God: (*Offstage*) This is my Son, whom I love; in him I am well pleased.

John: Well, I guess that answers my questions about your *ordinariness*, Lord!

Jesus: Bless you, John. Keep on doing what you were called by God to do, my brother. Now I'm off to do the same. (*Starts to exit stage right*)

John: Lord?

Jesus: (*Turns and looks back at John*) Yes?

John: Keep your eye on the ball and don't swing at the high hard ones!

Jesus: (*Scoops up a grounder and throws*) Gotchya!

(*Jesus, John, and Narrator exit*)

Epiphany 2
Isaiah 49:1-7
Psalm 40:1-10
1 Corinthians 1:1-9
John 1:29-41

An Epiphany For Simon Bar-Jona

Thespian Theological Thoughts

Simon Peter is one of my favorite people in the Bible, and I imagine he is for many of us stumble-bum males.

I recently read the following description of Peter: "Of volatile disposition, always meaning well, yet showing over-exuberance of spirit at times." That, in my opinion, is classic understatement. Peter was a fisherman: tough, profane, unrefined, unrestrained. Theology was not Peter's strong suit; in fact, he was probably illiterate. And Peter knew what he was: After he caught the miraculous net full of fish, Peter turned to Jesus and said, "Depart from me, Lord, for I am a sinful man."

But Jesus looked at Peter, and he saw something which even Peter himself couldn't see: He saw a heart full of love.

Peter continually got it all wrong: "Let's stay here on the mountaintop, and I'll make a tent for you, Lord." "You can't go to Jerusalem and be put to death, Lord!" "If you're going to wash my feet, wash all of me, Lord."

It has been said that, when Jesus said, "Upon this rock I will build my church," he must have been talking about Peter's hard head!

But Jesus did build his church upon Peter the rock! What about that? Peter's story tells me that Jesus can take *anyone* — even a hard-headed old stumble-bum like me — and accomplish his purposes ... as long as I will yield myself to him, and be teachable.

Cast
Narrator
Peter
Voice of Jailer (offstage)

(*Narrator is at podium stage left*)

Narrator: What image comes to mind when I mention the Apostle Peter? The rock on whom our Lord built his church? The Galilean fisherman who was called from his nets to become a "fisher of men"? The impulsive exuberant who never seemed to get it right? The braggart who claimed he would never forsake Jesus ... and the coward who did? The courageous leader of that small band of "followers of the Way" who transformed human history? Peter was all these, and more.

(*Peter enters slowly, stage right; he sits down center stage*)

Narrator: Here we see Peter at the end of his earthly life. He has been condemned to die, because he refused to quit proclaiming the Good News of Jesus Christ. Peter, I wonder if we could have a few words with you.

Peter: (*Looks up, startled*) Huh? Oh, sure. What can I do for you?

Narrator: Well, just a few questions for you. We want to understand you better.

Peter: What's to understand? I'm just a simple fisherman.

Narrator: But Jesus said you were the *rock* on which he was going to build his church!

Peter: I know ... Peter the rock: Isn't that amazing? Isn't *Jesus* amazing?

Narrator: Well, Peter, you *have* been something of a rock to this small band of Jesus' followers. You've been a courageous leader: you've refused to back down in the face of the Sanhedrin's insistence that you and your friends cease and desist from sharing Jesus with the people.

Peter: And look what that got me. Well, I guess they figured the only way to shut me up was to nail me up ... and so be it! I've done what Jesus asked me to do, and I'm not afraid to die.

Narrator: Pardon me, Peter, but things weren't always this way with you, huh? There was a time when you were very much afraid to die.

Peter: (*Puts his face in his hands*) Oh, yes. You don't have to remind me of that awful night: It haunts me still! (*Looks up*) The worst part of that memory is the way I shot off my big mouth to Jesus: "Oh, I'll never forsake you, Lord!" And then, before the night was over, I had done it three times ... what a hypocrite!

Narrator: But, Peter, today you are a hero of the faith. What made the difference in you?

Peter: Jesus!

Narrator: What do you mean? You had Jesus all along! When you denied Jesus, you had been with him for *three years*: You knew him as well as anyone on earth knew him, yet you denied him on the night he was arrested. Then, just a few weeks later, you're standing up to every authority on earth, boldly proclaiming Jesus as Lord. What happened to you?

Peter: *Jesus* happened to me.

Narrator: But ...

Peter: Let me finish. My experience of Jesus was *not* one big earth-shattering, blinding flash of light, after which I understood it all and believed it all. My experience of Jesus has been a *journey*.

Narrator: What do you mean? Tell us about it, Peter.

Peter: My journey started one day as I was returning from a long, hard day of fishing. My brother Andrew, who hadn't been with me that day, came and told me he had found the Messiah.

Narrator: What went through your mind when Andrew said that?

Peter: Look, my mind is a simple one; it doesn't have much room for theology. So, I have to tell you that, when Andrew came to me, what went through my mind was: "Okay, Andrew — you've been hanging out with that weirdo John the Baptizer, and now you've left him and found yourself another weirdo."

Narrator: What changed your mind, then?

Peter: Well, Andrew brought me to Jesus, and I met him face-to-face. And let me tell you, meeting Jesus face-to-face is an experience you never forget! He looked at me, and somehow I felt that he knew me and loved me better than I knew or loved myself. And then he told me: "You are Simon, the son of John; I'm going to call you the rock!"

Narrator: What did you think about that?

Peter: Frankly, I didn't know what to think. But there was something about this man that drew me to him ... and I couldn't walk away.

Narrator: So you decided to follow him?

Peter: I decided to see what he was all about. And over the following days and weeks, I began to realize that he was not like any other man I had ever met. He was *miraculous*: When my fisherman's luck gave out on me, he sent me back out to the same place where I had just got skunked and I caught a net-full of fish!

Narrator: So it was his miracles that drew you to him?

Peter: Not really. Miracles are nice, but they don't last. No, what really drew me to Jesus was ... well, it was just *Jesus*!

Narrator: You keep saying that. Can't you be a little more specific? We want something we can hold onto.

Peter: Specific? I don't know if I can do that. How do you put your hands around the wind? (*Pauses*) Well, I guess what drew me to Jesus was ... love.

Narrator: Love?

Peter: Yes, love. No-strings-attached love. When you are with Jesus, you really know what it is to be valued and loved for what you *are* ... not for what you *do*. I learned about that kind of love on the beach with Jesus, after the crucifixion.

Narrator: How so?

Peter: If Jesus loved me for what I *did*, would he still have wanted me to feed his sheep? I don't think so!

Narrator: You know, Peter, a lot of theologians are amazed that Jesus would have chosen *you* to feed his sheep. All the time you walked with Jesus, you didn't understand what he was doing, did you?

Peter: I sure 'nuff didn't. Man, if it had been up to me, Jesus and I would've camped out and had a picnic on that mountaintop with Moses and Elijah. But Jesus knew what he had to do, and he went and did it.

Narrator: And if he hadn't done it, you and I would be in a world of hurt, wouldn't we?

Peter: That's right. I understand that now, but I sure didn't get the picture back then!

Narrator: Speaking of that, Peter, there was another part of the picture you didn't get until much later.

Peter: You mean the part about the Messiah's mission, right? God says, "I will make you a light to the nations, so that my salvation may reach the ends of the earth." I have to admit it: I thought Jesus had come only to save the sons of Israel. It took a Roman centurion and the Holy Spirit to convince me otherwise.

Narrator: But to give credit where it's due, Peter ... you are teachable. You learned the lesson, and lived it.

Peter: Yup. I may not be the brightest bulb on the Christmas tree, but I am teachable. And I'm continuing to learn and grow, as I open my heart and mind to the Lord.

Voice of Jailer: (*Offstage*) Come, Simon Bar-Jona. It's time!

Peter: (*Starts to exit stage right*) Excuse me, I have to go now.

Narrator: One last question, Peter: What's the most important thing you learned in all your years of walking with Jesus?

Peter: Love. "You shall love the Lord your God with all your heart and with all your soul and with all your mind ... and you shall love your neighbor as yourself." Do this, and you will be doing what God wants you to do.

Voice of Jailer: Come on, Simon!

Peter: I'm coming, Lord, I'm coming. (*Exits right*)

Epiphany 3
Amos 3:1-8
Psalm 139:1-17
1 Corinthians 1:10-17
Matthew 4:12-23

Cliqueland

Thespian Theological Thoughts

If one or two of the caricature Christians in this play is uncomfortable for you, there are two options: (a) write it out of the play; (b) deal with it!

I pray that you will choose option (b), for we all need to deal with the sinful pride in ourselves which prevents our Lord's prayer in John 17 from becoming reality.

There are seven churches in this play; it just worked out that way. I don't know if that's significant, but I hope that the message is clear. If you have fun with it, maybe it will be clear.

Cast

Narrator
Do-Good Donald
   Church of the Doers of the Law
Heritage Harriet
   Church of the Children of Abraham
Bible-Thumpin' Betty
   Church of the Only True Word of God
Tongue-Wagging Thomas
   Church of the Spirit-Filled Prayer Warriors
Meditation Mildred
   Church of the Silent Servants of the Spirit
Cyberspace Cybil
   Church of the Eternal Internet
Flexible Fred
   Church of Anything Goes, Baby!

Seeker
Voice of God (offstage)

Props/Costumes
    Betty — Bible
    Thomas — prayer shawl
    Cybil — laptop PC
    Recording of lion's roar

(*Narrator enters stage right, and moves toward podium at stage left during opening monologue*)

Narrator: Once-upon-a-time, there was a town called Cliqueland. No, I didn't say "Cleveland," I said *Cliqueland*. As you may have guessed, the folks in this town were kind of a clubby bunch. They tended to gather and stay in little groups, and it seemed that each group took an extra serving of *pride* in itself. A funny thing about these groups: Each one of them called itself a *church*!

(*Do-Good Donald enters stage right*)

Narrator: Here comes one of them now: It's Do-Good Donald from the Church of the Doers of the Law.

Donald: "For not the hearers of the Law are just before God, but the doers of the Law will be justified" (Romans 2:13). Yes, my brothers and sisters: We must be *doers* of the Law. Get out there and *just do it* ... Swoosh! (*Makes a "swoosh" with his hand*)

(*Heritage Harriet enters stage left*)

Harriet: Heritage Harriet here to tell you that all that *doing* is so much hogwash, dahling! We at the Church of the Children of Abraham know that we are not justified by our doing: We are inheritors of the kingdom because we are all children of Abraham ...

praise God! (*Harriet and Donald pantomime an argument, upstage right*)

(*Bible-Thumpin' Betty enters stage right, carrying a huge Bible*)

Narrator: Oh-oh ... here comes Bible-Thumpin' Betty! I bet she's got something to say.

Betty: (*Thumps her Bible*) I sure do! It's all written here, in the precious and inerrant word of God. If he wrote it, I believe it, and that settles it. And at the Church of the Only True Word of God, we *know* who God is, and what he has to say. (*Thumps her Bible again*) It's all right here! (*Joins Donald and Harriet in the pantomime argument*)

(*Tongue-Wagging Thomas enters stage left; he is wearing a prayer shawl*)

Thomas: O thou great Jehovah: I beseech thee to hear me, and of thy great mercy pardon and deliver my brothers and sisters here from all their sins and wickednesses.

Narrator: Here's another citizen who always has something to say: Tongue-Wagging Thomas!

Thomas: And my brothers and sisters at the Church of the Spirit-Filled Prayer Warriors are continually lifting all you misguided heretics up in prayer, petitioning Almighty God that he might ...

All Others: Oh, give it a rest, Tommy! (*Thomas joins the pantomime argument*)

(*Meditation Mildred enters stage right*)

Mildred: M-m-m-m-m-m-m-m-m ... (*Sits down center stage, looks heavenward and continues humming*)

Narrator: Meditation Mildred! What are you doing?

Mildred: I'm doing what we at the Church of the Silent Servants of the Spirit do best: I'm meditating in peaceful silence ... m-m-m-m-m-m-m ... (*Gets up and moves upstage left, continuing to hum*)

(*Cyberspace Cybil enters stage left, carrying a laptop PC; she looks at Mildred as she passes and shakes her head*)

Cybil: (*Points to Mildred*) What a maroon! "Meditating in peaceful silence," indeed! Ya gotta be where the action is, Millie!

Narrator: Cyberspace Cybil! What's happenin'?

Cybil: The future! That's what's happening. (*Sits down center stage and opens her laptop*) At the Church of the Eternal Internet, we *always* know what's happening, and we're in touch with the Spirit of God in cyberspace.

(*Flexible Fred enters stage right*)

Fred: Cyberspace, shmyberspace! Ya gotta free your mind, baby!

Narrator: Now here's a real trip: Flexible Fred, from the Church of Anything Goes, Baby!

Fred: That's right: Anything Goes! Jesus has set us *free* — and we need to expand our minds and take in everything that freedom means. Don't be weighed down by the conventions of the past or the future. Be free! (*Starts a pantomime argument with Mildred and Cybil upstage left*)

Narrator: So that's the wonderful world of Cliqueland!

(*Seeker enters down center aisle*)

Narrator: And who are you?

Seeker: I'm a seeker.

Narrator: And what, pray tell, are you seeking?

Seeker: I'm seeking Jesus. I've heard that he has the truth.

(*One by one, the cast members move to center stage and chant their mantra three times; as each one finishes, he or she moves aside and continues to mouth the mantra silently*)

Donald: I am a Doer of the Law ...

Harriet: We are the Children of Abraham ...

Betty: (*Thumping her Bible*) God wrote it, I believe it, that settles it ...

Thomas: I pray to you, O Lord my God ...

Mildred: M-m-m-m-meditation, silent meditation ...

Cybil: Cyberspace is the space for me ...

Fred: Anything goes — I expand my mind ...

(*After Fred says his mantra, all seven surround Seeker, chanting their mantras louder and louder; Seeker looks around, confused; he covers his ears; finally, he shouts*)

Seeker: Quiet!

(*When quiet is restored, offstage Voice of God speaks*)

Voice of God: "Now I exhort you, brethren, by the name of our Lord Jesus Christ, that you all agree, and that there be no divisions among you."

All Seven: Huh?

Seeker: What's going on here? Who's got *Jesus* here?

All Seven: I do!

Seeker: What? Has Jesus been divided into seven parts?

All Seven: Huh?

Seeker: You can't all be right!

All Seven: (*Each points to self*) Yeah ... *I'm* right!

Seeker: (*Starts to exit down center aisle*) Well, I see that I won't find Jesus here! (*Exits*)

All Seven: (*Pointing at each other*) Well, now you did it: You drove away another seeker!

(*Offstage, a recording of a lion's roar is played; All Seven react in fear*)

All Seven: What's that?

Voice of God: The Lord God has spoken: Agree! No divisions among you! If you continue to promote your own personal views of me — each of you is wrong, by the way — you will continue to drive away all who seek me.

All Seven: But, but, but ...

Voice of God: No buts! Stop promoting *yourselves* and follow *me*. And realize that none of you has figured me out completely: You are *all* seekers ... got it?

All Seven: Got it, Lord.

Voice of God: Good! Now go, and sin no more.

All Seven: (*Put their arms around each other*) We're trying, Lord.

Voice of God: You certainly are: *very* trying! But I love you anyway.

(*All Seven sing "They'll Know We Are Christians By Our Love"*)

Epiphany 4
Micah 6:1-8
Psalm 37:1-18
1 Corinthians 1:18-31
Matthew 5:1-12

The Foolishness Of God

Thespian Theological Thoughts

Michael Card's wonderful song "God's Own Fool"[1] has long been an inspiration to me — because I'm a fool, you see. Card's lyrics show how Jesus played the fool to demonstrate that our assumptions and beliefs are often wrong and that much can be accomplished if, despite the seeming foolishness, we "believe the unbelievable" and become fools with and for Christ.

Cast

    Narrator
    Jesus
    Wilfred Whatchaknow
    Televangelist
    IRS Agent

Props/Costumes

    Jesus — fool's hat
    Wilfred — big book

―――――――――――――――

(Narrator is at podium, stage left)

Narrator: Jesus gave many teachings during his short stay here on earth, and one of his greatest was the Sermon on the Mount.

―――――――――

1. "God's Own Fool" by Michael Card, BirdwingMusic/Mole End Music.

(*Jesus enters stage left; he is wearing a fool's hat*)

Jesus: Blessed are the poor in spirit, for theirs is the kingdom of heaven.

(*Wilfred Whatchaknow enters stage right; he is carrying a big book*)

Wilfred: Now that is just plain foolishness! How can someone who is poor in spirit be "blessed" for Pete's sake?

Narrator: And who are you, with the big book there?

Wilfred: I am Wilfred Whatchaknow, that's who I am! And I am the Warden of the World's Wisdom — and *this* (*Lifts his book over his head*) is the Big Book of Beneficial Bodaciousness. It contains all the good stuff that I've learned — and recorded for posterity.

Narrator: My, my, that certainly is impressive!

Wilfred: Thank you.

Narrator: But let me get this straight: Are you saying that Jesus is talking foolishness here?

Wilfred: I certainly am!

Narrator: Whoa! You better watch your mouth, man! This is *Jesus*, ya know!

Jesus: Not to worry. For all my life, I've been called a fool — and much worse. But why do you think this is foolishness, Wilfred?

Wilfred: I told you: How can someone who is "poor in spirit" be considered *blessed*?

Jesus: Let me tell you a story. Two men went up to the temple to pray ... a televangelist ... (*Televangelist enters stage right*) ... and an IRS Agent. (*IRS Agent enters stage left*)

Televangelist: (*Looks heavenward*) Lord, I thank thee that I am not like other men ... especially this scum-bag IRS agent here, who keeps telling me that I owe more taxes! Lord, I fast and pray regularly ... and every Sunday, I am in the TV studio — oops, I mean church ... and I observe every letter of thy Law, Lord. Thank you, Lord, that I am holy!

IRS Agent: (*Looks downward*) Lord, have mercy on me, a sinner!

(*Televangelist exits stage right; IRS Agent exits stage left*)

Jesus: I tell you the truth: The sinner who knows he is a sinner went home justified before God ... he is "poor in spirit." Get the picture, Wilfred?

Wilfred: (*Writes in his book*) "The sinner who knows he is a sinner went home justified before God." Gotta take that down: that's *bodacious*!

Narrator: So, ya see? This isn't foolishness, after all!

Wilfred: Yeah, but what about the one about "the meek"?

Jesus: "Blessed are the meek, for they will inherit the earth."

Wilfred: Yeah, right! "The meek." What are those losers gonna *do* with the earth when they inherit it?

Jesus: Why do you call them "losers," Wilfred?

Wilfred: Well, because "the meek" always let others walk all over them, Lord. What good is it for *them* to inherit the earth anyway?

Jesus: Wilfred, my man, "meek" has nothing to do with the way you relate to others.

Wilfred: Huh? Whattaya mean?

Jesus: Could I have our friend the IRS agent back again, please?

(*IRS Agent enters stage left*)

IRS Agent: Lord, have mercy on me, a sinner. (*Exits stage left*)

Jesus: Wilfred, "meek" has to do with an attitude of humility toward *God*. Those who have a disposition of humility before God will inherit the land, and delight themselves in abundant prosperity. My main man David wrote that: It's in Psalm 37. Look it up, Wilfred!

Wilfred: (*Writes in his book*) "... delight themselves in abundant prosperity." That's *bodacious*!

Narrator: So, Wilfred: Have you changed your mind about the foolishness of Jesus?

Wilfred: W-e-e-e-e-l-l ... not yet! How 'bout this here now foolishness of yours about being "pure in heart"?

Jesus: Blessed are the pure in heart, for they will see God.

Wilfred: Yeah. What's that all about? I can't be "pure in heart" ... and I'm not even sure I *wanna* be!

Jesus: Why not, Wilfred?

Wilfred: Well, hey: That's a pretty harsh standard, "pure in heart." I think God expects too much of me with this "pure in heart" stuff, ya know?

Jesus: Here is what God expects of you, Wilfred: To do justice, and to love kindness, and to walk humbly with your God.

Wilfred: (*Writes in book*) That's it?

Jesus: That's it. A "pure heart" is a tough standard to meet, Wilfred — and I know that. You can't meet that standard on your own power — and I know that, too.

Wilfred: You do? Then why'd you lay that standard on us?

Jesus: So that you would lean on *me*, Wilfred. The Christian life is impossible without my help, but with me, all things are possible.

Wilfred: Hmmmmm ... (*Writes in book*) "With Jesus, *all* things are possible." That's *bodacious*!

Jesus: So, whatchathink, Mr. Wilfred Whatchaknow?

Wilfred: (*Sets down his book*) I think I'm gonna try relying on you, Lord. Your foolishness is starting to make more sense to me than all this here now beneficial bodaciousness! I've got a feeling the world isn't going to appreciate the Warden of Worldly Wisdom defecting to *you*, Jesus ... but ya know what? I don't care!

Jesus: Rejoice and be glad, for your reward is great in heaven.

(*Jesus and Wilfred exit stage left, arm in arm*)

Epiphany 5
Habakkuk 3:2-6, 17-19
Psalm 27
1 Corinthians 2:1-11
Matthew 5:13-20

The Lord Of The Way I Feel

Thespian Theological Thoughts

When I read the prayer of Habakkuk, immediately I heard a song by my favorite Christian musician, Don Francisco. The song is called "Jesus Is The Lord Of The Way I Feel," and it's based on the prayer of Habakkuk.

What I hear God saying to us through old Habakkuk is that *faith is not a feeling*. Faith is based on the eternal and unchanging word of God. So when our circumstances look bleak, and we *feel like* giving up, God says, "Don't waste your time worrying about your circumstances — trust me!"

That's not always easy for me to do, but if I really trust Jesus to be the Lord of my life, then he is The Lord Of The Way I Feel.

Cast

Narrator
Habakkuk
Voice of God (offstage)

Props

CD: *Don Francisco — The Live Concert*

(*Narrator is at podium stage left*)

Narrator: When your whole life seems to be a disaster, and your future looks as dark as the inside of your hat, can you praise the Lord anyway?

(*Habakkuk enters stage right*)

Narrator: Today we want to introduce you to a man who learned how to do that! His name is Habakkuk.

(*Habakkuk bows to the audience*)

Narrator: Funny name ... serious prophet! Habakkuk lived about 600 years before the birth of Jesus. As I said, he was a serious dude: He looked on the many sins of the people of Judah, and he complained to God:

Habakkuk: How long, O Lord, will you allow this wickedness to continue? Destruction and violence, strife and lawlessness! The wicked surround the righteous, and there is no justice! How long, Lord?

Voice of God: (*Offstage*) Glad you asked that, Habakkuk. Look around you and see what I am about to do: You won't believe your eyes! I am going to use the Chaldeans to punish the wickedness of the people of Judah. So there!

Habakkuk: The Chaldeans? Oh no, Lord — anything but the Chaldeans! Them guys is *mean*, Lord! Shoot, they're worse than the Judeans, for goodness' sake!

(*During the following speech, as God lists the characteristics of the Chaldeans, Habakkuk reacts to each statement with increasing fear and dread, as if he is being battered by God*)

Voice of God: Yup, fearsome they be, for sure. They march up and down the earth, seizing property.

Habakkuk: Oooh!

Voice of God: The Chaldeans fear no one; they are a law unto themselves.

Habakkuk: Eeeek!

Voice of God: Their horses are faster than leopards and meaner than wolves, and their horsemen ride in and devour everyone, taking and using captives like so much sand.

Habakkuk: Ow!

Voice of God: They laugh at fortresses and make fun of kings. The Chaldeans have no god except the strength of their arms.

Habakkuk: Oh, Lord ... not the Chaldeans! Where is the justice in punishing the wickedness of Judah by inflicting the Chaldeans on us? When the Chaldeans swoop down on us, it'll be like shooting fish in a barrel! Hey, Lord: Where's the justice in that? Them ol' Chaldeans are even more wicked than the people of Judah!

Voice of God: Your job is not to tell me about justice, Habakkuk. Your job is to write down the vision.

Habakkuk: What vision, Lord?

Voice of God: The vision of things to come, my son. Don't waste your time worrying about your current circumstances. Despite the way things may seem, I am still on the throne and in control.

Habakkuk: I wish I could believe that, Lord. But when I look around me, I feel like all is catastrophe! The people of Judah are wicked and corrupt ... but now you say you're sending the Chaldeans and their leopard-horses down on us. I feel like things are gettin' worser by the minute here, Lord!

Voice of God: Habakkuk, my son, are you my righteous prophet?

Habakkuk: Well, I *want* to be, Lord.

Voice of God: The righteous live by their *faith*. And faith rests not on human wisdom, but on the power of God.

Habakkuk: So, that's the vision, huh?

Voice of God: That's the vision: Trust me — I'm the real deal! Your circumstances are not the stuff of reality, because circumstances come and go. Only *I* am eternal and unchanging. Trust me! If you turn to me as your Lord, I will be Lord of your circumstances ... and Lord of the way you *feel* about your circumstances. Trust me!

(*Habakkuk kneels center stage*)

Narrator: The prayer of Habakkuk the prophet ...

(*Play "Jesus Is The Lord Of The Way I Feel" from Don Francisco's CD* Don Francisco — The Live Concert)

Habakkuk: (*After the song is over*) I will rejoice in the Lord; I will exult in the God of my salvation. God, the Lord, is my strength; he makes my feet like the feet of a deer, and makes me tread upon the heights!

Epiphany 6
Ecclesiasticus 15:11-20
Psalm 119:1-16
1 Corinthians 3:1-9
Matthew 5:21-24, 27-30, 33-37

Polly Pure And Righteous Rudy

Thespian Theological Thoughts

How can young people keep their way pure?

Better question: How can I (anything but a young person) keep my way pure? I have to tell you: When I read in Matthew 5 that Jesus says I'm committing *murder* when I call someone a bad name and *adultery* when I check out a pretty girl, I get nervous!

But I guess Jesus' point is that we need to do more than obey the letter of the law. If I bear such malice in my heart that I call my brother an evil name, I am murdering his spirit, even though I don't engage in the physical act of killing. And if I check out a pretty girl with lascivious thoughts in my heart, I am being unfaithful to my wife, even though I don't perform the act.

It's hard — no, it's impossible — to be pure. But that's the way God made us: We have to rely on him. And trust in his everlasting help and forgiveness and healing.

Praise God!

Cast

Narrator
Polly Pure
Righteous Rudy
Voice Of God (offstage)

Props

Polly — clipboard

(Narrator is at podium, stage left. Polly Pure and Righteous Rudy are seated in the audience: Polly at stage left, Rudy at stage right)

Narrator: How can young people — or anybody, for that matter — keep their way pure?

(Polly Pure and Righteous Rudy stand up and come to center stage)

Polly and Rudy: By guarding it according to God's word!

Narrator: Well, look what we have here!

(Polly stays center stage; Rudy moves upstage left)

Narrator: First, we have young Polly Pure: *(Polly curtsies)* Of her own righteousness she is sure!

Polly: Well, why shouldn't I be?

Narrator: Do you want me to answer that?

Polly: No, thank you. I want to answer your question: How can young people keep their way pure?

Narrator: And your answer is...?

Polly: By guarding it according to God's word ... like I do!

Narrator: And what do you mean by that, Polly?

Polly: Just treasure the word of God in your heart, you doofus! It's all so simple — I don't know why you can't grasp it, you numbskull!

Voice of God: *(Offstage)* Raca! Raca! Guilty!

Polly: (*Looks around, confused*) What? Who said that? Oh, well ... as I was saying when I was so rudely interrupted: All you have to do to keep your way pure is obey the Ten Commandments.

Narrator: And that's what you do, Polly Pure? (*Polly nods her head decisively*) Are you really, truly sure?

Polly: Of course I am, you nincompoop! (*Picks up clipboard and checks off each item as she recites*)
I have no other gods but Him;
I make no idol, bright or dim;
I never wrongly use God's name;
On Sabbath day I play no game;
I always honor mom and dad;
I've never murdered: that's *real* bad!
Adultery is beyond the pale;
I've never stolen — that's no tale!
I never lie, even when it's tough;
I covet not my neighbor's stuff!
... Am I sure I'm pure? You betcha!
And don't you forget it, dummy!

Voice of God: Raca! Raca! Guilty!

Polly: (*Looks around, confused*) Say what? Who's there? Well, anyway, that's it: All ya gotta know and all ya gotta do, to keep your way pure!

(*Rudy moves down to center stage*)

Rudy: That's right, sweet-cakes! (*Leers lasciviously at Polly*) All ya gotta do is live the righteous life.

(*Polly moves stage right*)

Narrator: Another country heard from! Ol' Righteous Rudy is truly a case: (*Rudy bows*) Self-righteousness radiates from his face!

Rudy: Yes, ma'am (*Leers at Polly again, then turns toward Narrator*) I'm here to tell ya, brother: the righteous life is the only life. Just live according to those ol' Ten Commandments, and your way will be pure. Hey, did ya get a look at *her* way? (*Points to Polly*) Va-va-vooom!

Voice of God: Cut out your eye!

Rudy: Say what?

Polly: He said, "Cut out your eye," dirt-bag!

Rudy: Huh?

Polly: So that you'll cease your adulterous ways, scum-bag!

Rudy: Adulterous ways? I'll have you know, young lady, that I have never cheated on my wife ... never!

Narrator: Then what's all this (*Imitates Rudy*) "va-va-vooom!" action, Rudy?

Rudy: Well, shoot. If a man can't *look* at a pretty girl, he might as well be dead, don't ya think?

Narrator: It's not what I think, Rudy.

Rudy: Huh?

Polly: It's what God's word says, you idiot! Treasure God's word in your heart, so that you may not sin against him.

Rudy: Oh, for Pete's sake, Polly! Don't be such a prude! (*Starts to exit stage right*) I can't waste my time with you anyway: I'm off to evening prayers. (*Exits stage right*)

Polly: Well, you'd better pray for forgiveness, you big dope!

Voice of God: Raca! Raca! Guilty!

Polly: Guilty? Who? Of what? (*Waits for an answer, gets none*) Well, I can't be bothered with all this foolishness: I'm late for prayer meeting. (*Exits stage left*)

Narrator: So, how can young people keep their way pure?

Voice of God: By guarding your way according to the word ... the living *spirit* of the word.

Narrator: As opposed to the *letter* of the word?

Voice of God: You got it, bubba! Now bring those two little "purists" back on stage, okay?

Narrator: Okay, Lord. Hey, Polly! Hey, Rudy!

(*Polly and Rudy enter*)

Polly: Hey, you loser! Why're you calling me back here? I've gotta get to my prayer meeting, ya know!

Rudy: Yeah, what's happenin' here? (*Leers at Polly, and pantomimes a "va-va-vooom!"*)

Narrator: The Lord has a few things to say to you guys.

Polly and Rudy: (*Look at each other, confused*) Say what?

Voice of God: I'd like to talk to both of you about keeping your way pure.

Polly and Rudy: Huh? We're pure, Lord!

Voice of God: I don't think so.

Polly: Excuse me? I have never broken any of your commandments, Lord.

Voice of God: How about Commandment Number Six, Polly?

Polly: (*Counts on her fingers*) Murder? I've never *murdered* anyone!

Voice of God: You keep calling people "numbskull" and "dirtbag," Polly. That's a violation of Commandment Number Six.

Polly: It is?

Voice of God: Yup! And if you're guilty of violating one, you're guilty on all counts.

Polly: Oooh!

Rudy: Looks like you're in big trouble, sweet-cakes!

Voice of God: Rudy, my man: Have you ever thought about Commandment Number Seven?

Rudy: (*Counts on his fingers*) Adultery? Excuse me, I have never — I repeat, *never* — cheated on my wife! Adultery, indeed!

Voice of God: What about "va-va-vooom," Rudy?

Rudy: What about it?

Voice of God: "Anyone who looks at a woman with lust has already committed adultery with her in his heart."

Rudy: Ooooh!

Polly: Now who's in trouble, scum-bag?

Voice of God: You two just don't get it, do you?

Polly and Rudy: Huh?

Voice of God: It's not enough to obey the letter of the law, folks: You have to obey the *spirit* of the law.

Polly: What do you mean?

Voice of God: "Murder" doesn't just mean killing someone. It includes murdering another's spirit ...

Polly: Huh?

Voice of God: ... by calling them "numbskull" or "dirt-bag."

Polly: Ooops!

Voice of God: And "adultery" isn't limited to physical contact. It includes what goes on in your mind, Rudy.

Rudy: Oooooops!

Narrator: Then how is it possible for *any* of us to keep our way pure?

Voice of God: You have to rely on me ... you can't do it alone!

Polly and Rudy: Well, we're trying, Lord.

Voice of God: You certainly are ... *very* trying! But I love you anyway!

Epiphany 7
Leviticus 19:1-2, 9-18
Psalm 71
1 Corinthians 3:10-11, 16-23
Matthew 5:38-48

You Shall *(OUCH!)* Be Perfect *(BRRR!)* As Your Heavenly Father *(OOOF!)* Is Perfect

Thespian Theological Thoughts

Be holy ... be perfect.

Lord, I can't do that!

Of course you can't. But take refuge in me, and I will be to you a rock (Psalm 71).

When I think of perfection, of course, I think of Jesus. And although Jesus was God incarnate, he "did not regard equality with God as something to be exploited ... and being found in human form, he humbled himself" (Philippians 2:6, 7).

It encourages me to know that Jesus was a man: a human being like me, with physical, mental, and emotional strengths and limitations like mine. Jesus' betrayal and arrest, the abandonment by his friends, and his trial and execution caused devastating physical, emotional, and mental anguish.

But Jesus wasn't devastated. Why?

Because he trusted and obeyed God the Father, and he relied on the guidance and comfort of God the Holy Spirit.

The same God who is still available to you and me, so that we may become "perfect, as your heavenly Father is perfect."

Cast

Narrator
Chris Chun
Private Enemy #1

Private Enemy #2
Private Enemy #3
Jesus

Props/Costumes

Private Enemies — t-shirt (or sign): "Private Enemy #1, #2, #3

Narrator — three signs: OUCH!, BRRR!, OOOF!; masking tape

Chris Chun — coat and sweater

Private Enemy #3 — suitcase, uniform and/or military hat

(*Narrator is at podium, stage left. Chris Chun enters stage left*)

Narrator: "You shall be holy, for I the Lord your God am holy." (*Chris looks up at the sky, bewildered*) "Be perfect, therefore, as your heavenly Father is perfect." (*Chris wrings his hands*) Behold my man Chris. (*Chris bows*) Chris Chun. Christ has just asked Jesus into his life, and now it appears he's a little confused about how Jesus wants him to live.

Chris: I'm not confused, I'm scared!

Narrator: Scared?

Chris: Yeah. How'm I gonna be "holy" and "perfect"? And what does that mean?

Narrator: Well, let's see ...

(*Private Enemy #1 enters stage left and approaches Chris*)

P.E. #1: Hey, dirt-ball, take this! (*Slaps Chris, backhand, across the right cheek*)

Chris: Why, you ...

Voice of Jesus: (*Offstage*) Ah-ah! Turn the other cheek, Chris Chun!

Chris: Huh? (*Looks around, confused*) Oh, yeah! (*Offers his other cheek; Enemy #1 slaps it, and exits stage left*)

Chris: Ouch!

(*Narrator takes sign: OUCH! and tapes it on front of podium. Private Enemy #2 enters stage right*)

P.E. #2: Hey, scum-bag! Gimme your coat, I'm cold.

Chris: Well, that's just tough ...

Voice of Jesus: Give him your cloak as well, Chris Chun!

Chris: Huh? (*Takes off coat and sweater*) Oh, yeah! (*Hands coat and sweater to Enemy #2, who exits*) Brrr!

(*Narrator takes sign: BRRR! and tapes it on front of podium. Private Enemy #3 enters stage left, carrying a suitcase. He wears a military uniform and/or a hat which signifies that he is a soldier*)

P.E. #3: Hey, doofus! Come with me a mile, and carry my luggage.

Chris: (*Looks skyward*) I know, I know: Go also the second mile. (*Picks up suitcase; it is very heavy, and he reacts to its weight*) Ooof!

(*Chris and Enemy #3 move stage right. Narrator takes sign: OOOF! and tapes it on front of podium*)

P.E. #3: Thanks, sucker. Adios! (*Exits stage right*)

Chris: (*Moves downstage left*) Man, this is hard! I gave my life to Jesus, and (*Points to podium*) look what it got me: OUCH! (*P.E. #1 enters and goes to center stage; Chris pantomimes being hit on cheek*) BRRR! (*P.E. #2 enters and goes to center stage; Chris pantomimes being cold*) OOOF! (*P.E. #3 enters and goes to center stage; Chris pantomimes lugging the heavy suitcase*) Look at what these scum-bags (*Points at Private Enemies*) have done to me! Yo, what's up with this Christian life, anyway?

Voice of Jesus: Love your enemies, and pray for those who persecute you.

Chris: Oh, maaaan! I can't do that.

(*Jesus enters stage right and moves to center stage. He puts his arms out as if being crucified. Private Enemies pantomime throwing dice for his clothes*)

Jesus: Father, forgive them; for they do not know what they are doing.

Chris: Yeah, yeah, I know, but, Lord, you were different from me.

Jesus: How so, Chris?

Chris: Well, you were the Son of God, the Messiah, the Chosen One.

Jesus: I *am* all that, Chris. But on the earth, I was also a man: a human being, just like you, with all the physical, mental, and emotional strengths and limitations that you have.

Chris: Huh?

Jesus: When they drove those nails into my hands and feet, that was a big OUCH! (*Takes down the OUCH! sign*) When Peter and my other friends deserted and denied me, there was a huge BRRR!

90

in my heart. (*Takes down the BRRR! sign*) And when I carried that cross the second mile — for you, Chris — that was an enormous OOOF! (*Takes down the OOOF! sign*)

Chris: Gee, Lord, I never thought about it that way. How did you do it?

Jesus: Through the power of the Holy Spirit, Chris.

Chris: See? I told you so: You *are* different from me. You've got the Holy Spirit goin' for you.

Jesus: Oh ... and you don't?

Chris: Huh?

Jesus: Chris, the Holy Spirit has always been there for you: the same Holy Spirit who comforted and strengthened me is yours for the asking. (*Hands the three signs to Chris*) And if you ask the Holy Spirit for help, you can *overcome* every OUCH! and BRRR! and OOOF! in your life.

Chris: I can?

Jesus: For sure. Give it a try!

Chris: Well, okay. Here goes: Come, Holy Spirit, and help me overcome the OUCH! in my life. (*Tears up the OUCH! sign, and hugs Enemy #1*) I forgive you, brother! Come, Holy Spirit, and help me overcome the BRRR! in my life. (*Tears up the BRRR! sign, and hugs Enemy #2*) I forgive you, brother! Come, Holy Spirit, and help me overcome the OOOF! in my life. (*Tears up the OOOF! sign, and hugs Enemy #3*) I forgive you, brother!

Jesus: Good for you, Chris! Now, keep working with us, and we'll make you:

Entire Cast: (*Together*) Perfect, as your heavenly Father is perfect!

Epiphany 8
Isaiah 49:8-18
Psalm 62
1 Corinthians 4:1-5 (6-7), 8-13
Matthew 6:24-34

Don't Worry ... Strive!

Thespian Theological Thoughts

How often we've heard it: "Don't worry!"

"Yeah, that's all right for *you* to say; you don't have to deal with my problems and temptations."

But we can't answer that way to Jesus, can we? "For we do not have a high priest who is unable to sympathize with our weaknesses, but we have one who in every respect has been tested as we are, yet without sin" (Hebrews 4:15).

My particular problems and temptations may not be solved as miraculously (and improbably) as Wilma's and Fred's are in this homily/drama, but one thing I know: God has inscribed me on the palms of his hands, and he will work things out to my eternal benefit.

And besides, I can't add a single hour to my span of life by worrying.

Cast

Narrator
Wilma Worrier
Fred Fretful
Fool
Voice of God (offstage)

Props/Costumes

Fool — fool's hat
Wilma — pay envelope
Fred — box labeled "Tenderloin Steaks"

(*Narrator is at podium, stage left*)

Narrator: This is a fable for the twenty-first century. It's the story of Wilma and Fred — no, not Wilma and Fred from *The Flintstones*. Meet Wilma Worrier (*Wilma enters stage right, moves to center stage and curtsies*) and her fiance, Fred Fretful. (*Fred enters stage left, moves to center stage and bows*) Wilma works as a widget winder at Walt's Widget Works. She gets paid minimum wage, and she feels she can't afford a decent dress for her wedding, unless she cheats on her time card, to make some extra money.

Wilma: Hey, ya gotta do whatchya gotta do, know-what'm-sayin'? And besides, Ol' Walt, that cheapskate, is payin' me starvation wages, fer-Pete's-sake, and he's gettin' rich off me! I don't feel one inch uneasy about gettin' a little of my own back from Walt!

Narrator: Well, um ... thank you for sharing that, Wilma. Now, let's meet Fred. (*Fred bows again*) He works as a Frank Filler for Frank's Fat-Free Franks. Fred feels that he doesn't make enough to feed himself *and* a wife, so he has to steal some of Frank's franks.

Fred: Hey, what's a few lousy tube steaks to a rich entrepreneur like ol' Frank? If that cheap dirt-ball paid me a decent wage, I wouldn't have to pay myself in tube steaks! (*Turns to Wilma*) Wilma, honey, I just don't know how we're gonna make it! Even with our combined paychecks, we can't feed and clothe ourselves and pay the mort-gage. (*Pronounces it "morte-gage"*)

Wilma: (*Wrings hands and gazes at Fred*) Oh, Fred!

Fred: (*Wrings hands and gazes at Wilma*) Oh, Wilma!

(*Fred and Wilma continue wringing hands and pace around stage*)

Narrator: Together now: One, two, three ...

Wilma and Fred: (*Face each other and hold hands*)
    Oh, woe is me!
    I cannot see
    How we'll ever
    Get together.

Wilma: (*Moves downstage right*)
    Winding widgets for Walt,
    I see my career at a halt!
    I won't be able to buy
    A wedding dress 'til I die.

Fred: (*Moves downstage left*)
    Frank's Franks —
    No, thanks!
    I'll never afford a wife:
    I'm doomed for the rest of my life!

Wilma and Fred: (*Face each other and hold hands*)
    Oh, woe is me!
    I cannot see
    How we'll ever
    Get together!

(*Fool enters down center aisle*)

Fool: Don't worry about your dress:
    God is bigger than your money mess!
    Don't worry about your meals:
    God is greater, and he heals
    All your woes
    From your head to your toes
    So ... don't worry!

Wilma and Fred: (*Together*) Who are *you*, for Christ's sake!

Fool: I am a fool for Christ's sake. And, for you, I have some of God's wisdom ... which is foolishness to the world.

Wilma: And God's wisdom is ... "Don't worry"?

Fool: Yup!

Fred: Well, that's okay for *you* to say, Fool! You don't have a mortgage to pay and a wife to support, and ...

Fool: How do you know what I have or don't have, Fred?

Fred: Er, well, I ... hey, how do you know my name?

Fool: I know your name, and I know your game, Fred!

Fred: Huh?

Fool: *Worry* is your game, Fred. And worry's gonna make you lame, Fred!

Fred: Oh, for — will you stop with the stupid rhymes, already?

Fool: Just tryin' to get your attention, bubba. You two have got to stop worrying. It'll kill you!

Wilma: But how are we ever gonna make it in this world, on our lousy paychecks?

Fool: Don't worry ... strive!

Wilma and Fred: Say what?

Fool: *Strive*, I say! Strive first for the kingdom of God and his righteousness, and all these things will be given to you as well.

Wilma: What in God's name does *that* mean, Fool?

Voice of God: (*Offstage*) One thing it means, Wilma, is not cheating on your time card.

Wilma: Huh? Who dat?

Voice of God: Who do you think would be speaking to you about the righteousness of God, Wilma:

Wilma: Oh-my-God!

Fred: Whoa ... God's gonna get you, Wilma!

Voice of God: Fred, my man, the righteousness of God also means not stealing Frank's fat-free franks from Frank.

Fred: Oooops! But, hey, how are we gonna make it, Lord? Run the numbers yourself: We don't have enough money to live.

Voice of God: Listen to the Fool, Fred. The foolishness of God is wiser than men.

Fool: I say again: Strive first for the kingdom of God and his righteousness, and all these things will be given to you as well.

Wilma: And *I* say again: What does that mean, Fool?

Fool: Why don't you try being an honest employee, Wilma? Walt might appreciate that. And, Fred, stop stealing Frank's franks, and you might be amazed at the things that'll be given to you.

Wilma: Well, okay. I'll try.

Fred: Me, too.

Wilma and Fred: (*Together*) But I don't know about this.

(*Wilma and Fred exit together stage right; Fool sits down center stage*)

Narrator: (*Pantomimes running fast*) Okay, now we fast-forward a couple of days. Wilma, with fear and trembling in her heart, has admitted to Walt that she's been cheating on her time card, and she has promised never to do it again.

(*Wilma enters stage right, holding her pay envelope*)

Wilma: I can't believe this! When I confessed to Walt and told him I'd never do it again, not only did Walt *not* fire me, he told me he was proud of me for being (*Makes quotation marks with her fingers*) "honest and courageous." And he said there'd be a surprise in my paycheck!

Fool: And what's your surprise, Wilma?

Wilma: I got a huge pay raise! More than I ever would've dared to steal from Walt. I can't believe it! (*Dances around happily*)

(*Fred enters stage right, carrying a box labeled "Tenderloin Steaks"*)

Fred: I can't believe it!

Fool: What can't you believe?

Fred: I went to Frank's office and told him that I've been taking tube steaks from him. I told him I was sorry, that I'll never do it again, and that I wanted to pay him back. And do you know what ol' Frank did?

Fool: I know, but why don't you tell us the story?

Fred: Well, Frank told me he was proud of me for being (*Makes quotation marks with his fingers*) "brave and forthright." And he gave me a raise! And then today, Frank gave me a *case* of tenderloin steaks — not tube steaks — for our wedding reception!

(*Fred puts down the box and he and Wilma dance around; when they stop dancing, they face the Fool*)

Wilma and Fred: (*Together*) I can't believe it!

Fool: Why can't you believe it? Don't you believe the wisdom of God?

Wilma: Well, yes ... but ...

Fool: But what?

Fred: Why would God reward us like this? Why would he even *care* about two petty crooks like me 'n Wilma?

Fool: Can a woman forget her nursing child, and have no compassion on the son of her womb? I will not forget you, says the Lord. I have inscribed you on the palms of my hands.

Wilma: Fred! We're inscribed on the palms of God's hands.

Fred: Well, praise the Lord, Wilma!

(*Fool brings Wilma and Fred to center stage; he puts one arm around each of them*)

Fool: So, what have you guys learned from this?

Wilma: I won't worry about my dress —
   God is bigger than my money mess!

Fred: I won't worry about our food —
God is *much* greater, dude!

Wilma and Fred: (*Together*) Don't worry ... strive!

Fool: For the kingdom of God and his righteousness.

(*Fool, Wilma, and Fred bow to the audience*)

Transfiguration Of The Lord
Exodus 24:12 (13-14), 15-18
Psalm 99
Philippians 3:7-14
Matthew 17:1-9

This One Thing I Do

Thespian Theological Thoughts

Saul of Tarsus was indeed a single-minded man. Hebrew of Hebrews, Pharisee of Pharisees, he had devoted his life to attaining the righteousness which comes from strict adherence to the Law.

And then he met Jesus.

All that is now rubbish to him ("dog dung," as one modern version puts it), compared to the surpassing value of knowing Jesus as Savior and Lord.

Now, that's an epiphany!

*   *   *

Some (you should pardon the expression) "thoughts" about producing this play:

- Three out of four ain't bad! I wrote Maryellen Moverandshaker into the play as the one who wouldn't repent. Please feel free to rewrite it and make any of the other three the unrepentant one.
- Henrietta, Peter, and Donald have several lines where, like Donald Duck's nephews, each character says only one or two words of the line. Have some fun with it!

Cast

Narrator
Henrietta Heroin
Peter Playboy

Donald Dotcom
Maryellen Moverandshaker
The Apostle Paul

Props/Costumes
 Henrietta — Sign: "DRUGS"/"JESUS"
 Peter — Sign: "SEX"/"JESUS"
 Donald — Sign: "MONEY"/"JESUS"
 Maryellen — Sign: "POWER"

(*Narrator is at podium stage left*)

Narrator: Today we have four stories for you. Our protagonists (that's a 64-dollar word for "lead characters") are people who are single-minded. Each one has a focus in his or her life, and that focus drives everything he or she does.

(*Henrietta Heroin enters stage right; she has a sign around her neck: "DRUGS"*)

Narrator: First, we have Henrietta Heroin. I guess I don't have to tell you what the focus of *her* life is!

Henrietta: (*Approaches Narrator threateningly*) Cut the sarcasm, bro'! Drugs are my thing, and I don't need any pious, preachy platitudes from you!

Narrator: Did I say anything pious or preachy?

Henrietta: Not yet. But I'll bet a dime bag of coke you were just about to start preaching at me about all my sins. Look, Homes, I'm a drug user, and I like it that way, okay? Drugs make me feel good, okay?

Narrator: Not okay, but I guess I know better than to argue with you at this point. My momma raised some ugly young'uns, but she didn't raise any fools!

Henrietta: Aaaah, what do *you* know, anyway.

(*Henrietta moves upstage left. Peter Playboy enters stage left; he is wearing a sign: "SEX"*)

Peter: (*To Henrietta*) Hey, sweet thing! What's up?

Henrietta: Hmmmm ... Well, honey, if you're up for a good time, then so am I. (*Puts her arm around Peter*)

Narrator: Now there's a match made in ... Well, wherever it's made, it's a classic match, that's for sure: Henrietta Heroin, whose life is focused on ... (*Henrietta proudly displays her sign*) ... and Peter Playboy, whose one thing is ... (*Peter proudly displays his sign*)

Peter: (*To Narrator*) So what's it to you, nosey-noodle? She likes drugs, I like her, and we both like havin' a good time. And we're not hurtin' anybody else. So just bug off, okay?

Narrator: Ummm ... okay. (*To audience*) Momma didn't raise no fools!

(*Henrietta and Peter exit together, stage left. Donald Dotcom enters stage right, wearing a sign: "MONEY"*)

Narrator: Ah, here's another tightly-focused piece of work. It's Donald Dotcom, entrepreneur par excellence.

Donald: Speak English, you doofus! I don't have time for all that high-falutin' French: I am about to become the most successful cyber superstar on the planet. Watch out, Bill Gates! Donald Dotcom is in the game now!

Narrator: Are you really that rich, Donald?

Donald: Yup! And when I close my next deal, I'll make Bill Gates look like a welfare case!

Narrator: What are you going to do with all that money, Donald?

Donald: Do? First, I'm gonna put major additions on my estates in Vail, and Newport, and the Italian Riviera, and Tahiti. And my Lear Jet fleet needs to be replaced: all eight of them are last year's models, and the ashtrays are full. And I've outgrown all my yachts: they need bigger flight decks for my helicopters. (*With a grand gesture*) And most importantly, some of my money will be used ...

Narrator: To feed and clothe the poor and shelter the homeless?

Donald: No, fool! To make *more* money!

Narrator: How much money is *enough* money for you, Donald?

Donald: Enough? I can't relate to that concept.

(*Maryellen Moverandshaker enters stage left. She wears a sign: "POWER"*)

Donald: Awwwriiight! Here's the lady who's gonna help me make it all happen: Maryellen Moverandshaker.

Maryellen: (*Gives Donald a big fake hug*) Huggie-huggie-kissie-kissie!

Donald: (*Disgustedly*) Yo, *that's* enough! Listen, Maryellen, have you got all the players together for my big merger?

Maryellen: Of course, daahhling! Just leave it to Maryellen. I've assembled the big-time players from Wall Street and Washington and a few Hollywood people just for good measure and I've got them all eating out of my hand. Ah, the precious perfume of per-spicacious power: it's so marvelously intoxicating. Don't you agree, daahhling?

Donald: Uhh ... sure, doll. Whatever you say. Can we get goin' here?

Maryellen: Certainly, daahhling. Come with me.

(*Maryellen and Donald exit together arm in arm, stage right*)

Narrator: Okay, now let's fast-forward in time. (*Acts out punching a fast-forward button, and then running fast*) Our four single-minded protagonists have tasted the fruits of their focused behavior — and now that they've eaten their fruit salad, our heroes don't look so good.

(*Henrietta enters stage left and moves to center stage; she is in bad shape*)

Henrietta: (*To Narrator*) Just shut up, okay? I don't want to hear your pious "I-told-you-so" sermon, okay?

Narrator: I didn't say anything about "I told you so," Henrietta. What happened to you, dear?

Henrietta: It's a long story, and you don't wanna hear it, and I don't wanna tell it. Let's just say the good times ran out, and I'm strung out. I think I need a methadone program.

(*Henrietta stumbles upstage left; Peter enters stage left*)

Narrator: Well, hello, Peter. What's up with you?

Peter: Nothing, and I mean *nothing*!

Narrator: So, your relationship with Henrietta didn't go anywhere?

Peter: Relationship? What relationship? And who's Henrietta, fer-Pete's-sake?

Narrator: Peter, Peter, Peter ... what's going to become of you?

Peter: I dunno, man. I'm tired of this life. The good times just aren't rollin' any more, know-what'm-sayin'?

(*Peter stumbles dejectedly upstage left and sits down next to Henrietta; neither one acknowledges the other. Donald enters stage right, holding his head in his hands*)

Donald: I can't believe it! I can't believe it!

Narrator: What can't you believe, Donald?

Donald: I can't believe my big deal fell through! I can't believe Donald Dotcom's stock price went into the tank! I can't believe all my creditors are calling their notes! I can't believe I'm going belly-up! And I can't believe I entrusted my future to that ditzy ding-bat Maryellen Moverandshaker!

(*Maryellen enters stage right*)

Maryellen: Who are you calling a ditzy ding-bat, you dorky doofus? I got all the big-time players together and *you* screwed it up with all your stupid charts and graphs. My friends were bored to death!

Donald: *I* screwed it up? Who were these bozos you brought to me, anyway? They couldn't see a good business deal if it was right under their noses! Some awesome arbitrageur *you* are!

Narrator: Arbitrageur? Hmmm. It seems you've got time for high-falutin' French now, Donald.

106

Donald: Oh, zip it up! (*To Narrator*) I've had it with you (*To Henrietta*) and especially with *you*, Ms. Maryellen Moverandshaker! (*Stomps upstage right and sits down*)

Maryellen: Well, I am ruined! All my influential friends have left me because of that insufferable boor. (*Points to Donald*) What am I to do?

Henrietta/Peter/Donald: What am *I* to do?

(*The Apostle Paul enters down the center aisle*)

Paul: Turn to Jesus!

Maryellen: And who are you, daahhling?

Paul: I am Saul of Tarsus, better known to you as Paul, an apostle of the Lord Jesus Christ.

Donald: (*Gets up and moves to center stage*) Whoa, the Apostle Paul! Now *there's* an impressive name for ya, Maryellen, you numbskull namedropper! (*Sticks out his tongue at her*)

Maryellen: (*To Paul*) Pay no attention to that dorky ding-bat, daahhling! (*Puts her arm around Paul*) Aaahhhh ... With *you* by my side, *real* power will be mine — er, I mean *ours*! And with my business and social connections — and your spiritual connection — we'll make a great team, don't you think, daahhling?

Paul: Well, not really, Maryellen. But I would like to talk to you about connections.

Maryellen: Yes, daahhling?

Paul: You know, Maryellen, before I met Jesus, I had a lot of those worldly power connections, too: I was of the tribe of Benjamin; I was a Hebrew of Hebrews; I was a respected Pharisee; I was — or

I thought I was — blameless before the Law. But today, I look at all that as *nothing*, compared to the joy and the power of knowing Jesus as my Savior and Lord.

Maryellen: Say what?

Paul: What I'm saying, Maryellen, is that worldly power is not what life is about.

Maryellen: Well, it may not be for you, daahhling, but I am still energized and excited by powerful friends. And I *will* have those friends back! All it'll take is a nice cocktail reception at the Haahvuhd Club. (*Strides confidently stage right*) Toodle-oo, daahhling! (*Exits*)

(*Henrietta stumbles down to center stage*)

Henrietta: Excuse me, sir. You were saying that life is not about power?

Paul: That's right, Henrietta.

Henrietta: Well, I've been sitting here nursing a hangover, and I've started thinking: Maybe life isn't about drugs, either.

Paul: Good for you, Henrietta!

(*Peter comes to center stage*)

Peter: Yeah. And you know, maybe life's not about sex, either.

Paul: Good for you, Peter. Praise the Lord!

(*Donald comes to center stage*)

Donald: Well, as one who's had it all and lost it all, I gotta tell you: Life isn't about money, either.

Paul: Well, good for you, Donald. Praise the Lord!

Henrietta: But
Peter: what *is*
Donald: life about?

Paul: Life is about knowing Jesus as Lord, counting all else as rubbish, and acknowledging that your righteousness and your worth as an individual come from Jesus, and from him alone.

Henrietta: That sounds nice, Paul, but I've been doing drugs for more than half my life. I'm a drug addict!

Peter: And I've been chasing women since I was in the fifth grade. I'm addicted to sex!

Donald: Uh-huh. And I've been making business deals since I played my first game of Monopoly. I'm addicted to money.

Paul: (*Points to Henrietta*) No, you're not! (*Points to Peter*) And no, you're not! (*Points to Donald*) And no, you're not! Each of you is a unique person, made in the image of God. And if you ask Jesus to be your Lord and Savior, you are children of God.

Henrietta: But
Peter: what about
Donald: my addiction?

Paul: Be addicted to Jesus!

Henrietta/Peter/Donald: Huh?

Paul: Listen to me, you three: As addicts, you were single-minded, right? Henrietta, everything you thought and did was focused on getting drugs, right?

Henrietta: I guess you could say that.

Paul: And Peter, your life was totally focused on chasing women, right?

Peter: That's for sure!

Paul: And Donald, all you've ever thought about was money, right?

Donald: Ya got that right!

Paul: So you — all three of you — are very focused, single-minded people. What you need to do now is make *Jesus* and his will for you the focus of your lives.

Henrietta: Man,
Peter: that's
Donald: harsh!

Paul: You may think so, but you can do it. If I can do it, you can do it.

Henrietta/Peter/Donald: Huh?

Paul: Before I met Jesus, I was single-minded like you. My whole life was focused on righteousness according to the Law ... so much, in fact, that I persecuted and executed the followers of Jesus. But Jesus got my attention — in a way I think you'd call "harsh" — and ever since then, I have been single-minded in a new and better way. *This one thing I do:* forgetting what lies behind (like drugs, sex, and money), I press on toward the goal: Jesus, my Lord and Savior.

Henrietta: And that's
Peter: all there is
Donald: to it?

Paul: That's it. And the Holy Spirit is always there to help you do it — so just do it! (*Makes a "swoosh" with his hand*)

Henrietta: Well,
Peter: we'll
Donald: try!

(*Henrietta, Peter, and Donald turn their signs around to reveal "JESUS" on the reverse*)

Donald: But what about Maryellen, Paul? She didn't seem to want to admit that she needs Jesus.

Paul: Hey, three out of four isn't bad! You just leave Maryellen to me, Donald. I haven't given up on her yet. Remember, I'm a single-minded guy!

Henrietta: That
Peter: you
Donald: are!